TARNISHING OF THE BADGE

JERRY SUMMERS

DEDICATION

To the men and women who courageously wear the law enforcement uniform, honoring it daily with pride, integrity, and guts that so few understand and many don't appreciate. Thank you for your sacrifices.

CONTENTS

LAW ENFORCEMENT CODE OF EHTICS

Fundamental Duty. As a law enforcement officer, my fundamental duty is to serve the community; to safeguard lives and property; to protect the innocent against deception, the weak against oppression or intimidation, and the peaceful against violence or disorder; and to respect the Constitutional rights of all to liberty, equality and justice.

Personal and Official Life. I will keep my private life unsullied as an example to all and will behave in a manner that does not bring discredit to me or my agency. I will maintain courageous calm in the face of danger, scorn, or ridicule; develop self-restraint; and be constantly mindful of the welfare of others. Honest in thought and deed in both my personal and official life, I will be exemplary in obeying the law and the regulations of my department. Whatever I see or hear of a confidential nature or that is confided to me in my official capacity will be kept ever secret, unless revelation is necessary in the performance of my duty.

Appropriately Enforce the Law. I will never act officiously or permit personal feelings, prejudices, political beliefs, aspirations, animosities or friendships to influence my decisions. With no compromise for crime and the relentless prosecution of criminals, I will enforce the law courteously and appropriately without fear or favor, malice or ill will, never employing unnecessary force or violence and never accepting gratuities.

Public Trust. I recognize the badge of my office as a symbol of public faith, and I accept it as a public trust to be held so long as I am true to the ethics of law enforcement service. I will never engage in acts of corruption or bribery; nor will I condone such acts by other law enforcement officers. I will cooperate with all legally authorized agencies and their representatives in the pursuit of justice.

Professional Performance. I know that I alone am responsible for my own standard of professional performance and will take every reasonable opportunity to enhance and improve my level of knowledge and competence. I will constantly strive to achieve these objectives and ideals, dedicating myself before God to my chosen profession…law enforcement.[1]

---

[1] Idaho POST, "POST Council's Code of Ethics," Accessed August 11, 2016,
https://www.post.idaho.gov/ProfessionalStandards/documents/POST%20Council%20Code%20of%20Ethics.pdf

CHAPTER 1

THE CRISIS DEFINED

"The police are the public and the public are the police."
Sir Robert Peel

In 2011, while writing my MBA dissertation, I observed that law enforcement was on the cusp of a crisis in regards to public trust, branding, and the industry's ability to self-police. Today, law enforcement and the jurisprudence system within the United States have become the target and primary focus of local and national news media organizations. Sensational headlines involving corruption, abuse of power, and official misconduct are a continuous source of public concern. This crisis has highlighted a growing distrust of the professional standing and reputation of the law enforcement and judicial systems. Technological advances in police equipment, protocols, and procedures, along with the increasing mobilization of society, have resulted in the isolation of individual officers from those they serve during regular non-enforcement interactions. According to Sir Robert Peel, the ability of police services to function appropriately in performance of their duties requires the publics' approval of law enforcement actions.[2] While the public trust crisis doesn't rest entirely on the backs of law enforcement professionals, they have not been without error and fault in its creation.

Decades ago, individual police officers recognized that their badge was

---

[2] Bloy, M., (2010) 'Sir Robert Peel's Nine Points of Policing', *A Web of English History*, [Online] Available From: http://www.historyhome.co.uk/peel/laworder/9points.htm (Accessed 3 March 2011).

a symbol of the public's trust and, because of that trust, their personal motivations, attitudes, biases, and prejudices were subject to intense public scrutiny. This fact, which is not fully appreciated by some officers today, was fully disclosed to all of them upon their affirmation of the Law Enforcement Code of Ethics. (**Please** take the time to read it at the beginning of this book.) Within this context, an officer voluntarily accepts public scrutiny when he/she agrees to keep their private life unsullied and to live as an example to others regarding personal integrity and compliance with the law. The public trust and statutory authority bestowed upon police officers should and does require a higher standard of individual performance. Those not wishing to be subjected to such public scrutiny have always had and continue to have the option of choosing a different career path. Once one recognizes, and accepts, that the fundamental reason for law enforcement's existence is service to the community then it's easy to understand that the natural consequence of losing this focus will always be a corresponding loss of public trust and organizational credibility. Looking back over the years, one can clearly see that this subtle shift away from self-policing and holding officers involved in malfeasances to the established standards of the Law Enforcement Code of Ethics has diminished the profession's image and reputation, resulting in a severe distrust of law enforcement nationwide. My opinion, from personal and professional experience, is that violations of The Law Enforcement Code of Ethics are not being enforced to the extent outlined in the code. Fundamentally, officers are:

"To keep their private lives unsullied and to serve as examples, not to discredit themselves or their agency.

To be honest in their thoughts and deeds in both their personal and professional life.

To be exemplary in obeying the law and to maintain the confidences given to them.

Not to act officiously, or allow prejudices, political beliefs, personal feelings, aspirations, animosities or friendships to influence their decisions.

To recognize the symbol of public faith and trust their badge represents.

Not to condone acts of corruption, bribes, or any such acts when committed by other police officers.

To be responsible for their own competency, conduct, and professional performance."[3]

---

[3] Gerald A. Summers, "Law Enforcement Decertification: Shifting the Paradigms of Ethics, Morality, And Politics from Law Enforcements' Traditional Approach to A Resource-based View" MBA diss., University of Liverpool, 2011.

These requirements are not being upheld to the extent the profession professes, demonstrating a systematic failure in law enforcement's role in self-policing coupled with an unawareness or denial of the effects of negative word of mouth communication. The devastating effects of negative word of mouth have been clearly witnessed in the rhetoric of the Black Lives Matter movement. Their slogan, "hands up don't shoot," coined in the Michael Brown shooting in Ferguson Missouri, enflamed public opinion and consciousness and remains a powerful call to action today, even though an independent forensic investigation revealed that narrative was not accurate. Yet, since the Michael Brown shooting, this slogan has been seen in peaceful and violent protests involving police behaviors in the Freddie Grey, Alton Sterling, and Philando Castile cases, even before any investigation had been conducted. It was seen most recently during the protest that culminated in the killing of multiple police officers in Dallas, Texas. The insufficient understanding or denial of the public perception's influence on the reputation and image of law enforcement indicates the need to shift paradigms from current approaches.

One of the major components to any organization's success is how the inevitable service failures are handled. Traditionally, police services have looked to officer decertification as the primary response to officer malfeasance, ignoring the factors of agency reputation, public image, public trust, and ultimately the corresponding public's view of the agency's credibility. The failure of some police administrators to recognize the importance of developing their agency's reputation with respectable mayors and city council members to garner deep community support has diminished their organization's ability to manage or capture the synergistic benefits of local business's "interdependencies and complex relationships."[4]

Research conducted by Rindova, Williamson, Petkova and Sever (2005 cited by Boyd, Bergh and Ketchen, 2010) suggests that organizational reputation is comprised of two distinct dimensions: "quality rooted in economic orientation and market prominence based upon sociological tradition with precursors that include the media, expert affiliations and premiere organizational status."[5] For police, possessing a reputation for providing a quality service has a direct correlation to sustainable taxpayer funding based upon the local business community and citizens' desire to

---

[4] Boyd, B., Bergh, D., & Ketchen, D., (2010) 'Reconsidering the Reputation-Performance Relationship: A Resource-Based View', *Journal of Management*, 36 (3), pp. 588-609.

[5] Boyd, B., Bergh, D., & Ketchen, D., (2010) 'Reconsidering the Reputation-Performance Relationship: A Resource-Based View', *Journal of Management*, 36 (3), pp. 588-609.

influence elected officials on the police departments' behalves. A department's prominence within the community enables the development of long-term synergistic affiliations, strengthens internal employee market orientation, enhances selection/recruitment programs, and enables greater flexibility for service recovery options. Application of these principles over the years has been minimal within the police services industry, to its own detriment.[6] Instead, many people within police departments today view the media, elected officials, and business owners input as nuisances to be placated through an "us versus them" mentality.

The most prolific research conducted on police malfeasance issues during the last two decades has been accomplished by Roger Goldman and Steven Puro (1987, 1997, 2001). They initially joined efforts in 1987 while examining police decertification in light of the United States Supreme Court decision in *Mapp v. Ohio* for dealing with evidence suppression based upon police misconduct or illegal police action, commonly known as the 'exclusionary rule.' The courts have consistently recognized the need to deter police misconduct and have steadfastly resisted becoming "accomplices in the willful disobedience of a Constitution they are sworn to uphold." The courts also simultaneously prevented police profiting "...from its unlawful behavior, thus minimizing the risk of seriously undermining popular trust in government." Clearly, the courts have recognized the inherent necessity for governmental transparency and the absolute mandate for law enforcement to maintain public trust in the policing of its own profession when dealing with an officer's inappropriate behaviors and actions.

The exclusionary rule's design and purpose was to eliminate or prevent police misconduct in gathering evidence during the investigative process. Goldman and Puro argued individual states can accomplish essentially the same result as the exclusionary rule through effective revocation of individual officers' certification when misconduct merits. Without state certification, it is impossible to be employed as a police officer. Goldman and Puro further submitted that revoking an officer's certification would have a greater impact than termination from employment given the high probability an officer terminated from one agency would find work with another in the same state.[7] While termination is an effective strategy and

---

[6] Gerald A. Summers, "Law Enforcement Decertification: Shifting the Paradigms of Ethics, Morality, And Politics from Law Enforcements' Traditional Approach to A Resource-based View" MBA diss., University of Liverpool, 2011.

[7] Goldman, R., & Puro, S., (1987-1988) 'Decertification of Police: An Alternative to Traditional Remedies for Police Misconduct', *Hastings Constitutional Law Quarterly*, 15 (45), pp. 45-80.

position to take, personal experience demonstrates few Peace Officer Standards and Training (POST) decertification boards have the political will to remove an officer's right to work, especially if the officer's employing agency failed to appropriately discipline the officer's misconduct. This failure demonstrates the need for intermediary disciplinary protocols, including the ability of POST boards to publicly censure or suspend officer certifications for a specific period of time, except in the most severe of circumstances.

While the exclusionary rule worked for the courts in suppressing wrongfully or illegally obtained evidence, it didn't eliminate the officer's right to remain employed in his/her chosen profession. A violation of the fourth amendment on the part of individual police officers does subject the department and governing jurisdiction, as well as the individual, to potential criminal prosecution and civil ramifications via Title 42 of the United States Code, Section 1983.[8] Goldman and Puro focused on police decertification as a mechanism to eliminate the probability of recurring misconduct by a specific officer while ignoring the need for individual agencies and the law enforcement industry to maintain, and even enhance, its reputation and public image. In order to improve upon the public's trust, the application of appropriate systems (such as public disclosure of disciplinary results) must be established to demonstrate to the community that department management does hold offending officers responsible for their malfeasance.

While one cannot dispute the effectiveness of Goldman and Puro strategy in preventing a particular officer from perpetuating recurring incidents, it is seen as addressing only the symptoms of the problem and not effectively addressing or correcting the underlying causes. Often, decertification is viewed as the only remedy for preventing similar recurrences without the progressive and corrective actions of education, counseling, censure, license suspension, and remedial training being employed prior to officer decertification.[9]

In an updated 1997 study, Goldman, Puro, and Smith completed research on police decertification for the decade covering 1985-1995. Extensive statutory improvements had occurred during this timeframe with states previously lacking revocation authority having gained such authority.

---

[8] Goldman, R., & Puro, S., (1987-1988) 'Decertification of Police: An Alternative to Traditional Remedies for Police Misconduct', *Hastings Constitutional Law Quarterly*, 15 (45), pp. 45-80.

[9] Gerald A. Summers, "Law Enforcement Decertification: Shifting the Paradigms of Ethics, Morality, And Politics from Law Enforcements' Traditional Approach to A Resource-based View" MBA diss., University of Liverpool, 2011.

Their study, still focusing on decertification as the major remedy for officer malfeasance, specifically sought to answer whether states had a broad, narrow, or unchanged decertification authority. Broad authority was defined as POST having the authority to revoke officer certifications for convictions or subsequent plea bargains for crimes designated as a felony and misdemeanor crimes involving moral turpitude, as well as Code of Ethics violations, incompetence on the part of the officer, dishonesty in one's official capacity, and dependence on drugs or alcohol.[10] Narrow authority was defined as POST lacking the ability to revoke police certifications for unspecified acts or omissions. Generally, Goldman, et al. found "...the more specific a statute is in defining revocation offenses, the more limited the POST authority becomes in revoking an officer's certification."[11] One improvement during this and subsequent decades came from reporting requirements obligating chiefs and sheriffs to report all changes in employment status and any misconduct of their officers involving state statutes, POST regulations, and Code of Ethics violations, to the state certifying agency. The second improvement came in the form of qualified immunity for agency heads who report officer misconduct to POST. Without qualified immunity, many agency administrators feared retribution from their officers in the form of civil litigation claiming defamation.[12] Today, however, in most states, disclosure of officer misconduct is still shrouded in mystery, protected as private personnel matters, and not subject to public disclosure. A crucial element in gaining public trust for law enforcement is transparency and disclosure in regards to specific officer behaviors and actions, whether deemed positive or negative. This type of information should be subject to public disclosure. The law enforcement and judicial community must eventually acknowledge and acquiesce to its customers and stakeholders needing transparency in all aspects of policing and criminal justice if each of these professions is to gain trust, respect, and confidence from the public they must serve.[13]

---

[10] Puro, S., & Goldman, R., & Smith, W., (1997) 'Police decertification: changing patterns among the states, 1985-1995' *Policing: an International Journal of Police Strategies & Management*, 20 (3), pp. 481-496.

[11] Puro, S., & Goldman, R., & Smith, W., (1997) 'Police decertification: changing patterns among the states, 1985-1995' *Policing: an International Journal of Police Strategies & Management*, 20 (3), pp. 481-496.

[12] Puro, S., & Goldman, R., & Smith, W., (1997) 'Police decertification: changing patterns among the states, 1985-1995' *Policing: an International Journal of Police Strategies & Management*, 20 (3), pp. 481-496.

[13] Gerald A. Summers, "Law Enforcement Decertification: Shifting The Paradigms of Ethics, Morality, And Politics From Law Enforcements' Traditional Approach to A Resource-based View"

By 2001, Goldman and Puro had recognized that forty-three of the fifty state POST Academies had been granted statutory revocation authority. They concluded law enforcement's approach of leaving officer misconduct disciplinary procedures to agency administrators had failed because of the administrator's inability or refusal to appropriately address or terminate officers for malfeasance. But once again, they failed to consider implementing intermediary disciplinary steps of education, counseling, censure, certification suspensions, and remedial training prior to officer decertification. Goldman and Puro began calling for a mechanism, either on a state or national level, for certification revocation. While improvements had been made regarding POST certification and revocation authority, many states were beginning the contrary process of reducing this revocation authority, and attempts were initiated to classify POST Academy as an educational facility versus a certification agency. Inconsistencies regarding officer selection and acceptance criteria, which involved factors that eliminated individuals from being granted entry into a POST Academy for certification purposes, were not being considered as grounds for decertification for officers that had already received state certification.[14] More specifically, officers committing offenses that prevented individuals from gaining state certification were not decertified. The effect of these inconsistent decisions and actions by POST academies and decertification boards across the United States continued to erode the public's trust in law enforcement's ability to self-regulate, which damaged the industry's reputation and public image.[15]

Next Goldman and Puro began calling for a National Decertification Database (NDD), containing the names of officers who have been decertified. Since no federal agency felt compelled to establish or monitor such a database, the International Association of Directors of Law Enforcement Standards and Training (IADLEST) created such a database. As of this writing, only a handful of states are supplying such information, which allows all POST Directors instant access to the basic information for those individuals whose state certification has previously been revoked. This information is critical in minimizing the possibility of decertified officers

---

MBA diss., University of Liverpool, 2011

[14] Goldman, R., & Puro, S., (2001) 'Revocation of Police Officer Certification: A Viable Remedy for Police Misconduct', *Saint Louis University Law Journal*, Spring 2001.

[15] Gerald A. Summers, "Law Enforcement Decertification: Shifting The Paradigms of Ethics, Morality, And Politics From Law Enforcements' Traditional Approach to A Resource-based View" MBA diss., University of Liverpool, 2011

receiving certification from another state's POST Academy.[16] It is intriguing that only a handful of states are supplying decertification information to IADLEST when the topic of certification revocation is consistently one of the most wrestled with dilemmas facing the fifty POST Directors, especially since there *was* agreement by most of the IADLEST members to create a decertification database. The failure of a majority of members to provide information to the database brings into question law enforcement's true motivation for self-policing. This fact has further eroded public trust and fueled the demand for greater transparency regarding officer malfeasance and police disciplinary actions.[17]

The importance of developing strong relationships with citizens is a critical function of government recognized by da Silva and Batista. They pointed out the existence and importance of lifetime relationships beginning at birth and terminating with death. This point is especially poignant as it relates to police services, in which both occurrences, birth and death, have occurred as a direct result of specific police actions. Each of these instances has the potential of dramatically affecting the department's reputation both positively and negatively. It was also noted in their research that there is a general citizen belief that government is abusing its power, causing citizens to disengage politically for fear of retaliation from those in positions of authority. This fear further exacerbates the commonly held belief that government is corrupt, wasteful, inefficient, or totally ineffective in providing adequate services in exchange for the revenue it receives. Public sector employees are often viewed as rude, lazy, and lacking in any customer service initiative. These attitudes often become polarized when dealing with citizens' relationships with the police. News coverage of police corruption furthers these stereotypes, which are then intensified by the law enforcement profession's reluctance to take appropriate disciplinary action against its own members. It is to the shame of law enforcement that so many administrators consistently fail to recognize or acknowledge the idea that an organization's reputation "embodies the history of people's experiences with the service provider."[18]

---

[16] Goldman, R., & Puro, S., (2001) 'Revocation of Police Officer Certification: A Viable Remedy for Police Misconduct', *Saint Louis University Law Journal*, Spring 2001, 15.

[17] Gerald A. Summers, "Law Enforcement Decertification: Shifting The Paradigms of Ethics, Morality, And Politics From Law Enforcements' Traditional Approach to A Resource-based View" MBA diss., University of Liverpool, 2011

[18] da Silva, R., & Batista, L., (2007), Boosting government reputation through CRM', *International Journal of Public Sector Management*, 20 (7), pp. 588-607.

It is equally important for citizens to realize that the law enforcement function is fraught with contradictions. Officers are instructed to be culturally sensitive, politically correct, polite in their speech, firm in their presence, authoritative when gaining control of a situation, and directive in others movements. Officers are required to have the patience of Job, the communication skills of a great mediator, and still keep themselves and others safe and out of harm's way in some of the most vile and demanding situations. As human beings, officers are subject to the same feelings and emotions as the citizens they serve. There will be times when they will lack compassion, become cynical and skeptical of others, and lack tact or an appropriate demeanor. It is usually during times of extremely high stress that a police service failure occurs.

How a service failure is handled by police supervisors and administrators is critical to a police organization's reputation and public image. Administrators, being far removed from the incident, have the ability to recover from real or perceived officer failures without criticizing the individual officer. When an officer failure occurs, the administrator can view the failure from the victim's perspective and address the issue appropriately. If an apology is needed, they apologize. If some action is left undone, they make sure it gets completed in a timely manner.[19] Service recovery systems are designed to bring healing for a strained relationship between a customer and an organization while providing another opportunity to correct a customer's bad image of an organization.[20] In this case, it would be a citizen's image of the police organization.

According to research, the greater freedom an employee is granted in solving a customer's problem without supervisory interference, the better the service recovery system's performance becomes. Furthermore, it has been noted the more authoritative the management hierarchy was, the weaker the employee became producing service recovery solutions.[21] This single factor is key for law enforcement supervisors and administrators to understand and adjust to. In a profession where a paramilitary chain of command approach thrives, frontline, boots-on-the-ground officers are

---

[19] Gerald A. Summers, "Law Enforcement Decertification: Shifting The Paradigms of Ethics, Morality, And Politics From Law Enforcements' Traditional Approach to A Resource-based View" MBA diss., University of Liverpool, 2011

[20] Lin, W.B., (2010) 'Relevant factors that affect service recovery performance', *The Service Industries Journal*, 30 (6), pp. 891-910.

[21] Lin, W.B., (2010) 'Relevant factors that affect service recovery performance', *The Service Industries Journal*, 30 (6), pp. 891-910.

reluctant to address minor problems and correct them. Instead, the trained response is to kick the problem up to the sergeants' level for resolution. While this may be the correct organizational response, it runs counter-intuitive to an effective service recovery system. Administrators of police services beginning to understand these principles better will allow greater flexibility for the individual officers to address and correct minor failures on the street, thus eliminating the need for the citizen to complain. As the issues are appropriately addressed and resolved at the lowest possible level within the police organization, it will become more likely that the police organization will be viewed by its community as responsive to citizen's concerns and progressive in its management. The single question a police supervisor or administrator should ask themselves and their subordinates is how will the anticipated action consistently earn the public's trust?

Does a moral and ethical void currently exist within the law enforcement industry? Have self-regulation and the primary service recovery system failed in the area of compliance to the standard set through the established and universally accepted Law Enforcement Code of Ethics? I contend that, categorically, self-regulation has failed at every level of the industry, with the only exception being for the most egregious of violators. Furthermore, given the current level of regulation within the law enforcement industry, why are our regulators, administrators, POST directors, and decertification board's compliance alarms not speaking out in protest? And, if they are, why aren't these problems being resolved? I believe law enforcement and the American justice system is now becoming embroiled in an ethics and morality crisis tantamount to that of the United States banks in "2008 after the collapse of Lehman Brothers ... [in which] the survival of the financial system hung by a thin thread of trust ... almost completely torn apart by the magnitude of the crisis."[22] This type of unethical behavior is easily explainable when leaders in a particular industry do "not subscribe to the stakeholder approach," as in the current actions and make-up of the law enforcement and justice system.[23]

As an illustration of a failure to the stakeholder approach, in a July 4, 2011, Los Angeles Times article, Joel Rubin claimed a 2008 disciplinary process instituted by the Los Angeles Police Department was failing to hold

[22] Gerald A. Summers, "Law Enforcement Decertification: Shifting the Paradigms of Ethics, Morality, And Politics from Law Enforcements' Traditional Approach to A Resource-based View" MBA diss., University of Liverpool, 2011.

[23] Rossi, C., (2010) 'Compliance: an over-looked business strategy' *International Journal of Social Economics*, 31 (10), pp 816-831.

officers involved in malfeasance accountable for their actions. The procedure in question was called a "conditional official reprimand." It meant that in many cases, misconduct that once brought suspension without pay would bring a warning that future offenses will bring severe penalties. In 2008, 14 officers were issued these simple reprimands, but the total jumped to 109 in 2010. Apparently, these reprimands were being issued to officers who had been convicted of serious criminal violations such as driving while intoxicated, domestic violence, excessive use of force, and even in circumstances involving racial slurs. In a public meeting, a police commissioner questioned Deputy Chief Perez about the ethics of the program. Perez was head of the Professional Standards Division and responsible for designing the program. The commissioner's concern was that "the way [the new disciplinary procedure is] being handled minimizes the seriousness of these situations." These sentiments were echoed by the commission president, who claimed that "we need to make sure that this process does not distort our value system."[24]

LAPD officials seem to have taken the stance that there is no need for definitive boundaries or guidelines for these reprimands because they want flexibility in executing officer discipline.[25] Understandably, the current citizen oversight isn't accepting this lack of definitive boundaries. In a police organization fraught with past serious ethics violations (for example, the Rampart Division scandal; the widely publicized Rodney King beating; and the locker room racial slur revealed during the O.J. Simpson trial) insistence upon no definitive consequences for officer malfeasance gives the appearance of a cultural practice in law enforcement often referred to as the "thin blue line," where officers will either claim no knowledge of a questionable behavior or outright lie for another officer, claiming a fictional set of circumstances. Furthermore, my professional experience demonstrates the power of the complete opposite. When definitive guidelines are set and adhered to via progressive disciplinary procedures, officer compliance becomes second nature and an organizational culture of ethics and morality becomes the norm. This, of course, requires management consistency, and involves countless officer terminations for those who refuse to comply with the department's expectations and

[24] Rubin, Joel, (2011) 'New discipline policy at LAPD results in some officers avoiding punishment' *The Los Angeles Times*, [Online] Available From: http:// www.latimes.com/news/local/la-me-lapd-reprimand-201110704,0,6772068.story (Accessed 10 August 2011).

[25] Rubin, Joel, (2011) 'New discipline policy at LAPD results in some officers avoiding punishment' *The Los Angeles Times*, [Online] Available From: http:// www.latimes.com/news/local/la-me-lapd-reprimand-201110704,0,6772068.story (Accessed 10 August 2011).

standards. Initially, retention rates drop, but morale improves as the ethical officers support management's adherence to established professional standards. The lack of perceived consistency pointed out in this article highlights the culture of the law enforcement profession and its willingness to hold citizens to a higher standard than they hold themselves. Is it any wonder law enforcement is experiencing branding and trust issues from those they have sworn an oath to treat fairly and impartially? It becomes especially offensive to the general public, because officers have promised to be exemplary in obeying the laws they enforce. For over two decades, scholars and law enforcement professionals have pointed out these types of short-comings and wrestled with mechanisms to best solve failures on the part of the law enforcement industry. While this article is directed towards the LAPD, these issues and responses are not isolated. It doesn't matter the size of the police organization; all police agency's wrestle with the same issues in policing. Progress has been made, but the key issues remain and haven't been appropriately addressed. Confusion still abounds with what the primary function of police services are today. I suggest many helaw enforcement woes can be resolved by simply returning to our original function of customer service by recognizing that the very survival of police services depends on public support.

It is apparent that an enormous dichotomy exists between how law enforcement views itself and how the public views law enforcement. The results above clearly indicate law enforcement professionals view themselves as possessing a reputation for trustworthiness, yet media portrayals indicate a branding and public image crisis that doesn't uphold that reputation for police service organizations.[26] A lack of effective communication skills continues to plague the police services industry even though it has been estimated that 97% of all police work requires effective communication and the more accommodating the officer appears, the higher the likelihood of perceived trust on the part of media and the general public.[27] If nothing else, the previously discussed Los Angeles Times article highlights the reasons for police organizations to consider shifting paradigms from their current approach to problem solving. Organizational systems are analyzed and given credibility based upon their merits, not the

---

[26] Gerald A. Summers, "Law Enforcement Decertification: Shifting the Paradigms of Ethics, Morality, And Politics from Law Enforcements' Traditional Approach to A Resource-based View" MBA diss., University of Liverpool, 2011.

[27] Myers, P., Giles, H., Reid, S., & Nabi, R., (2008) 'Law Enforcement Encounters: The Effects of Officer Accommodativeness and Crime Severity on Interpersonal Attributions are Mediated by Intergroup Sensitivity', Communication Studies, Vol. 59, No. 4, October-December 2008, pp. 291-305.

good old boy approach of "this is the way we've always done things around here." The 'good old boy' approach isn't working and needs to be changed. Those within the profession can choose to bring about changes voluntarily or it will be required of them by external forces.[28]

It is not too late for the law enforcement profession to "transpose the analogies and lessons learned," return to a more traditional and stricter adherence to the Law Enforcement Code of Ethics, and rebuild the public trust lost over the last two decades. Police departments must acquire and adhere to an understanding that "reputations are crucial when decisions are being made" in relation to officer disciplinary actions and/or decertification.[29]

---

[28] Gerald A. Summers, "Law Enforcement Decertification: Shifting the Paradigms of Ethics, Morality, And Politics from Law Enforcements' Traditional Approach to A Resource-based View" MBA diss., University of Liverpool, 2011.

[29] Rossi, C., (2010) 'Compliance: an over-looked business strategy' *International Journal of Social Economics*, 31 (10), pp 816-831.

CHAPTER 2

A POLICE OFFICER'S WORLD VIEW

"We sleep safely at night because rough men
stand ready to visit violence on those who would harm us."
Winston S. Churchill

The previous chapter was critical of the law enforcement profession due to the shortcomings noted above. This chapter will address the failings of mayors, city council members, and community members. As a sergeant in 2004, I distinctly remember attending the training, "Recognizing, Understanding, and Managing the Problem Public Safety Employee," taught by Kevin M. Gilmartin, Ph.D. Dr. Gilmartin spent twenty years in law enforcement prior to beginning a career as a behavioral scientist. As a scientist, he now works at helping police officers understand and deal with the internal and external personal and professional attacks that often change idealistic young officers into cynical, angry individuals. At the very beginning of the class, he utilized an exercise where he had the class write down their first thought in response to a word or phrase. This exercise was especially revealing because of the difference in responses between police management and human resources professionals. The phrase used was "Boy Scout Leader." The cops in the room responded with terms like pedophile, molester, pervert, and various other similar terms while the non-law enforcement professionals responded with terms like, individual who likes children, good citizen, and other complimentary terms. Dr. Gilmartin then asked the non-law enforcement professions if they thought the cops had a warped worldview, and most felt the cops' view of the world was indeed warped, cynical, and out of touch with reality.

To my surprise, Dr. Gilmartin agreed with the non-law enforcement professions in their opinion of police. However, he then he asked those individuals how many of them, by a show of hands, hesitated in the doorway

interview. Not placing her under oath allowed him to later admit she had, in fact, lied to the FBI during the investigation (but he was under no obligation to file charges because she hadn't been under oath). Secondly, Director Comey admitted that this candidate disclosed classified information to individuals who lack the security clearances to receive such information, which is also a crime.[32] From my perspective, based on his public reiteration of the things Hilary Clinton did and didn't do, Director Comey's failure to recommend charges to the Department of Justice constitutes a violation of the Law Enforcement Code of Ethics and demonstrates how little significance the Code of Ethics plays in law enforcement today. This colossal breach at the highest levels of law enforcement, and subsequently the United States government, has further sullied the profession's reputation. As a former chief of police, I understand some of the pressure that must have been on Director Comey, but he had a job to do and personal and professional integrity to protect, and in my opinion he failed miserably to uphold that integrity.

On a personal level, I can understand why he chose the path he did. After all, integrity in politics and higher levels of government is rare these days. Had he taken the ethically different path, the powers-that-be would have crushed him and ruined his career, and in the long run probably very few individuals would have cared. I know from personal experience what it means to hold an individual in a higher position of authority than yourself accountable and have them end your career and damage your retirement. Even though I prevailed through the Federal Court System, I was still not made whole. But in the situation I was in, it was my duty to adhere to the law enforcement oath I took. If we, as leaders in law enforcement, wish to regain the public's trust we must always do the ethical thing, even if it is the hard thing. Director Comey, in this instance, failed to apply the law fairly, equally, and impartially without deference to political and social standing, as required by the oath he took so many years ago. If the head of one of the most respected agencies within the federal government will subvert the Law Enforcement Code of Ethics without repercussions, why should any street level police officer hold those standards in high regard? The only reason that high standards will ever occur is if the leadership of each agency demands it, and then backs those demands by example and with disciplinary procedures that are consistent and may include disciplinary actions including termination for such blatant ethical violations.

The fact that multiple excuses have been made for Director Comey by

---

[32] James Comey, House Oversight & Government Reform Committee, Representative Trey Gowdy (R-SC) Questions FBI's Director Comey, July 7, 2016, (C-Span.org).

senators and congressmen indicates the level of corruption now acceptable within the hallowed halls of government. Is it any wonder the American people are near all-out anarchy? Unfortunately, this type of scenario is played out daily within government not only at the national level, but also on the state and local levels. The American people deserve better. They deserve honesty, integrity, and ethical behavior from our political leaders, but instead of demanding that level of behavior from themselves, it is easier for our political leaders to shift the blame onto the ones duty bound to hold society accountable: the men and women of law enforcement. However, this time, the repercussions for this blame shifting are worse than ever expected. A war on law enforcement has been declared, promoted by uninformed, race baiting civic leaders, politicians, and even the president of the United States. Complacency is a poison administered one drop at a time, and unfortunately it has been administered to the American people in a steady drip for the last two decades. Now, hatred for police officers regardless of race, color, gender, or sexual orientation has boiled over to the point that officers are hated simply because they wear a uniform. Hatred for others is just as sharply present when people are divided along lines of color and ethnicity by ignorant leaders who refuse to educate themselves appropriately of the facts before spouting off about racism, police brutality, constitutional violations, or policing procedures.

At this point, it's no longer a matter of education, because political and civic leaders for the most part are more interested in promoting their own narrative, whether it's accurate or not. Years ago, the courts developed a reasonable officer standard which became the methodology used to determine how reasonable officers, with like training and experience, would react in a similar situation to see if a particular officer's actions were prudent and acceptable. This standard is critical to understand when analyzing police behavior, because most citizens do not have the ability to view potential threats through the same lens as a trained officer. Many police administrators and supervisors have invited, suggested, even pleaded with elected officials to attend the department's citizens academy to gain a greater understanding of police protocols, procedures, and actions. In my personal experience with this, all the elected officials refused to complete a citizens academy which only required ninety minutes a week for twelve weeks. As part of this academy the officials would be required to ride along with an officer for one session. The elected officials told me they didn't have the time, but upon receiving a citizen's complaint about an officer, they would require detailed information which they would have already had knowledge about had they completed the citizens academy curriculum. This complete lack of commitment on the part of elected officials, and subsequent questioning of an officer's judgment, often created animosity between officers and elected officials, with the officers viewing the constant questioning of their actions not only as a lack of support for the department, but also for individual officers.

In short, government has experienced a systemic failure in relation to ethics, integrity, and honesty resulting in chaos. Unless community, political, and law enforcement leaders are willing to join in a concerted effort to understand the complexities of police work without judging or attempting to shift the blame, along with fully educating themselves about the facts before reacting to politically charged issues, this lack of trust from community members is going to escalate into more frequent violent encounters. All sides have a major stake in solving these complex issues, and all sides have culpability in the system's failure. Refusal to listen to one another with the purpose of understanding, rather than responding, will only promote greater disparity.

Finally, it is important to point out that it is a citizen's duty to comply with a lawful directive from a police officer. Many will insist officers violate individual rights and, as such, compliance isn't required. Let me be clear on this fact: it is not only prudent but also necessary for a citizen to fully comply with the orders of a police officer for the safety of everyone involved in the situation. Failure to do so is an unlawful act. There are administrative and legal remedies for individuals, whose rights have been violated by overzealous officers, but the moment when tensions are high and violence could be one wrong move away is not the time to argue. Compliance is always the best option for everyone's personal safety, and it is the law.

CHAPTER 3

A COMPARISON IN LEADERSHIP

"The only thing necessary for evil to triumph
is that good men do nothing."
Edmund Burke

During the writing of this book, the massacre of five police officers in Dallas, Texas occurred near the conclusion of a Black Lives Matter protest. I was impressed by the true courage and leadership of Chief David Brown of the Dallas Police Department that showed in the way he handled this tragedy. In a major city that has dealt with racial tensions for decades, Chief Brown's leadership, management, and community policing philosophy have been a calming influence, especially when in the middle of this horrendous event. Chief Brown maintained transparency in the midst of chaos. His vulnerability, and ultimately his courage, in disclosing the fact that the shooter, Micah Johnson, was killed by the Dallas Police Department when they sent in a robotic bomb in order to safeguard the officers,[33] was perhaps the most transparent disclosure in law enforcement I can remember. In a profession where many police administrators attempt to sequester such details, the citizens of Dallas need to recognize the honesty and courage of their current chief of police. There is a tendency for people, when left with a void of information, to fill that void with negative assumptions. They imagine all sorts of events and circumstances, often asking what the department has to hide and why they won't disclose more information to

---

[33] Chief David Brown, Press Conference, Dallas Police Used Bomb Robot To Take Down Gunman Who Shot Cops, NBC News Special Report, July 8, 2016.

the citizens. It is always a tenuous balance for a chief to maintain the integrity of the investigative process while also supplying adequate information to the community and media.

Chief Brown's approach has been to engage and incorporate the community in problem solving. This model was recognized for its success in February 2013 when the Dallas Morning News ran an editorial in which the conclusion read, "Just coincidence that crime and tensions are historically low in Dallas? I think not. Under Brown's leadership DPD has focused on strategies that pay off."[34] Additionally, Chief Brown challenged the protestors to make a difference in their neighborhood, when, in June of 2016, he said, "We're hiring. Get off that protest line and put an application in and we'll put you in your neighborhood and we will help you resolve some of the problems you're protesting about."[35] Immediately after the chief's call to action, job applications rose 344 percent, according to the Washington Post.[36] Once again, Chief Brown demonstrated how transparency in government is supposed to work. It's fine to raise awareness, but it's *better* to be part of the solution.

In stark contrast to Brown's leadership, we find the leadership style of President Obama. The men are similar. Both are African American, close to the same age, and both hold positions of power. While Chief Brown attempts to unify individuals, even those who initially oppose him, President Obama, who has raised many valid points in recent speeches, has failed, in my opinion, to unite opposing sides and has actually divided individuals along racial lines. After the shooting death of Trayvon Martin and subsequent acquittal of George Zimmerman, President Obama said, during a press conference on July 19, 2013:

> "There are very few African-American men in this country who haven't had the experience of being followed when they were shopping in a department store. That includes me. There are very few African-American men who haven't had the experience of walking across the street and hearing the locks click on the doors of cars. That happens to me -- at least before I was a senator. There are

---

[34] Sharon Grigsby, "Dallas DPD Chief Brown's toolbox of community policing pays off", The Dallas Morning News, February 19, 2015.

[35] Richard Fausset, Alan Blinder, and Manny Fernandez, "Dallas Police Chief, David O. Brown, Is Calm at Center of Crisis, The New York Times, July, 11, 2016.

[36] Jacob Bogage, "The Dallas police chief told protesters to apply for police jobs. Now, job applications are up 344 percent," The Washington Post, July 28, 2016.

very few African-Americans who haven't had the experience of getting on an elevator and a woman clutching her purse nervously and holding her breath until she had a chance to get off. That happens often.

And I don't want to exaggerate this, but those sets of experiences inform how the African-American community interprets what happened one night in Florida. And it's inescapable for people to bring those experiences to bear. The African-American community is also knowledgeable that there is a history of racial disparities in the application of our criminal laws -- everything from the death penalty to enforcement of our drug laws. And that ends up having an impact in terms of how people interpret the case."[37]

Then, after the Eric Garner decision by a Grand Jury not to indict Officer Daniel Pantaleo for the strangulation death of the suspect during the arrest of Mr. Gardner who was selling unstamped cigarettes outside of a convenience store in New York, President Obama, speaking at the 2014 White House Tribal Nations Conference, delivered the following statement: (Please note that President Obama indicates the grand jury had everything on video, and he still questioned their decision not to indict.)

"Some of you may have heard there was a decision that came out today by a grand jury not to indict police officers who had interacted with an individual with Eric Garner in New York City, all of which was caught on videotape and speaks to the larger issues that we've been talking about now for the last week, the last month, the last year, and, sadly, for decades, and that is the concern on the part of too many minority communities that law enforcement is not working with them and dealing with them in a fair way.

And there's going to be, I'm sure, additional statements by law enforcement. My tradition is not to remark on cases where there may still be an investigation. But I want everybody to understand that this week, in the wake of Ferguson, we initiated a task force whose job it is to come back to me with specific recommendations about how we strengthen the relationship between law enforcement and communities of color and minority communities that feel that bias is taking place; that we are going to take specific

---

[37] President Barrack Obama, Remarks by President on Trayvon Martin, James S. Brady Press Briefing Room, July 19, 2013.

steps to improve the training and the work with state and local governments when it comes to policing in communities of color; that we are going to be scrupulous in investigating cases where we are concerned about the impartiality and accountability that's taking place.

And as I said when I met with folks both from Ferguson and law enforcement and clergy and civil rights activists, I said this is an issue that we've been dealing with for too long and it's time for us to make more progress than we've made. And I'm not interested in talk; I'm interested in action. And I am absolutely committed as President of the United States to making sure that we have a country in which everybody believes in the core principle that we are equal under the law.

So I just got off the phone with my Attorney General, Eric Holder. He will have more specific comments about the case in New York. But I want everybody to know here, as well as everybody who may be viewing my remarks here today, we are not going to let up until we see a strengthening of the trust and a strengthening of the accountability that exists between our communities and our law enforcement.

And I say that as somebody who believes that law enforcement has an incredibly difficult job; that every man or woman in uniform are putting their lives at risk to protect us; that they have the right to come home, just like we do from our jobs; that there's real crime out there that they've got to tackle day in and day out -- but that they're only going to be able to do their job effectively if everybody has confidence in the system.

And right now, unfortunately, we are seeing too many instances where people just do not have confidence that folks are being treated fairly. And in some cases, those may be misperceptions; but in some cases, that's a reality. And it is incumbent upon all of us, as Americans, regardless of race, religion, faith, that we recognize this is an American problem, and not just a black problem or a brown problem or a Native American problem.

This is an American problem. When anybody in this country is not being treated equally under the law, that's a problem. And it's my job as President to help solve it."[38]

Then after the initial reports of the Alton Sterling and Philando Castile shootings, but before initial investigations had even been completed, President Obama said, in a speech given from Warsaw, Poland:

"But what I can say is that all of us as Americans should be troubled by the news. These are not isolated incidents. They are symptomatic of a broader set of racial disparities that exist in our criminal justice system.

And I just want to give people a few statistics to try to put in context why emotions are so raw around these issues. According to various studies, not just one, but a wide range of studies that have been carried out over a number of years, African-Americans are 30 percent more likely than whites to be pulled over.

After being pulled over, African-Americans and Hispanics are three times more likely to be searched. Last year, African-Americans were shot by police at more than twice the rate of whites.

African-Americans are arrested at twice the rate of whites. African-American defendants are 75 percent more likely to be charged with offenses carrying mandatory minimums. They receive sentences that are almost 10 percent longer than comparable whites arrested for the same crime.

So if you add it all up, the African-American and Hispanic population who make up only 30 percent of the general population make up more than half of the incarcerated population. Now, these are facts.

And when incidents like this occur, there's a big chunk of our fellow citizenry that feels as if because of the color of their skin, they are not being treated the same. And that hurts. And that should trouble all of us.

This is not just a black issue. It's not just a Hispanic issue. This is an American issue that we should all care about, all fair-minded people should be concerned."[39]

---

[38] President Barrack Obama, Remarks by the President at the Tribal Nations Conference, accessed August 9, 2016. http://www.whitehouse.gov/the-press-office/2014/12/03.

[39] President Barrack Obama, President Obama on the Fatal Shootings of Alton Sterling and Philando Castile, July 8, 2016. http://medium.com/the-white-house/president-obama-on- the-fatal-shootings-of

Finally, on July 14, 2016, in a town-hall-style meeting, President Obama defended the Black Lives Matter Movement by saying, "Because of the history of our country and because of the images we receive when we we're growing up, et cetera, often there's a presumption that black men are dangerous, so that has to be worked through."[40]

I believe the president is correct in stating that this isn't a black or Hispanic or white issue. It is an American issue. But then why, as a Harvard educated attorney, is he making such statements about being fair-minded *prior* to the investigative process being complete? And why is he questioning the validity of the process when the results have not been fully vetted?

While I can acknowledge and even agree with President Obama, as he has raised concerns about inconsistencies and valid failures within the American jurisprudence system, I believe he has misstated the root cause of these disparities. While the president sees these issues as stemming from a racial cause, I see it more as an economic issue. These problems go so much deeper than race. Throughout our county's history there have been tremendous atrocities committed against the economically disadvantaged. Some examples are African-American and Chinese-American slavery, the imprisonment of Japanese citizens during World War II, and discrimination against women, Italian immigrants, Polish immigrants, Irish immigrants. There are more examples, I'm sure; too many to name.

Individuals who are economically disadvantaged tend to do anything necessary to provide for their families, including sometimes committing crimes. This problem is further exacerbated when the economically disadvantaged are educationally disadvantaged as well. Yet, what all of these other ethnicities did to slow and even reverse the tide of discrimination and oppression was to work within the system of the new society they found themselves in. As a specific ethnic community, they organized and developed community leadership to work on their specific concerns within the American jurisprudence system, raised social awareness about specific concerns for their ethnicity, and ultimately found ways to hold wayward members of their community accountable for inappropriate actions. When necessary, that included cooperation with law enforcement. I believe we fail our citizens, regardless of skin color, when we reduce our current problems to that of race. Furthermore, even within the president's position on this topic there are significant contradictions.

Where is his sense of outrage regarding white privilege when it comes to his former Secretary of State? Where is the transparency in his

---

[40] Julie Hirschfeld Davis, "Obama Warns of Growing Mistrust Between Minorities and Police," The New York Times, July 14, 2016.

administration that he promised the American public? If he is so outraged about racial disparities in the United States, why isn't he doing anything about the appearance of impropriety in the meeting between his attorney general and former President Bill Clinton prior to FBI Director Comey's recommendation not to file charges against Hillary Clinton? The general consensus seems to be that if something like that had happened on a state or local level, President Obama would be calling for a federal investigation. Yet the American public is supposed to take what is said about this very suspicious meeting at face value? Should we not consider that the president had just claimed that American law enforcement and the American judicial system is unfair and biased, and favors white people? Might I be so bold as to suggest the problem of corruption originates at the top of the food chain and is infused throughout all aspects of government, law enforcement, and the judicial system based on the acts of those in the highest positions of power? If, as President Obama so eloquently pointed out, that as President of the United States this is his problem to fix, why has he not led by example and addressed this appearance of unseemliness within his own administration? I leave it to you to form opinions about that question.

CHAPTER 4

THE SIMPLICITY OF COMPLIANCE

"The more I learn about people, the more I like my dog."
Mark Twain

Recently there has been a lot of discussion about non-compliance and refusal to follow what has been perceived as unlawful orders by police officers. In every U.S. state, there is a law which prevents citizens from resisting, delaying, or obstructing an officer in the performance or attempted performance of the officer's duty. In other words, it is illegal to resist, obstruct, or delay an officer in the performance of duty. Now, before we get into a circular discussion of what is the lawful performance of one's duty and whether it is appropriate to disobey, let me start by pointing out that if the officer is violating someone's constitutional rights, there are other avenues within the American judicial system to appropriately address that issue. Therefore, there is absolutely no reason not to comply with the direction of a police officer. If those directions are determined later to be unlawful, then your recourse is through litigation, not heat-of-the-moment non-compliance, which will more likely than not lead to an arrest in which force is met with force.

As a citizen, you may feel justified in resisting, but to do so will most likely result in charges being filed against you and an increased level of force to gain compliance, which I have already said is absolutely necessary in a police officer's line of duty. In law enforcement, this reality is known as the use of force continuum. Hypothetically, let's assume all the accusations levied against law enforcement officers today are true. If there truly is a national crisis in police racism and excessive use of force, why on earth would anyone ever fail to comply with an officer's instructions? If the police are truly brutalizing minorities, why would anyone of color ever fail to comply? Simple logic would require self-preservation, which would dictate a different response, because the expectation would always become the reality, and injury or death would always be the expected outcome for non-compliance.

If we let go of the completely pessimistic assumption from above, it's clear that the majority of police officers are not racist, brutalizing thugs; they are hard working men and women of all colors, genders, and sexual orientations entrusted by their communities and states to faithfully uphold and enforce all laws, from their local jurisdictions, to the Constitution of the United States. They are asked to do so without prejudice, bias, animosity, or favoritism, and are color blind in the law's application. However, I'm not so naïve as to assume there are no bad cops. There are, and it is the obligation of other officers and police administrators to weed them out of the profession quickly. Most do, but the cold hard truth is that there are some that do not, for many reasons. For example, some administrators know that if they fire a cop the elected officials won't replace that officer. Some administrators, who are being proactive and effective in removing bad apples, will come under intense scrutiny by a media that questions their management ability due to the increased turnover rates under their leadership. It is also unfortunate that, in most jurisdictions, those in police management are prohibited from disclosing the outcomes of administrative reviews and internal affairs. This is because any action taken to correct or remove the problematic officer is protected by union representatives and employment laws as being a personnel matter and not subject to public disclosure. I have taken a more controversial view and believe that, as public employees, any investigative action should be disclosed at the conclusion of the investigation to the general public, for two reasons. First, a public employee's salary is paid by tax dollars collected in the community and, as such, I believe that the public deserves full disclosure of its "employee." Second, this also allows for citizens to review the actions of the administrators to determine how effectively they are holding their employees to the acceptable policies, procedures, and standards of their profession. Too often police management, union representatives, and elected officials hide their inaction or inappropriate action toward employee misconduct within the veil of confidential personnel matters. In essence, this unwillingness to hold their employees to a high standard actually condones the malfeasance.

Many in public service will protest loudly, because employees within the private sector aren't subjected to such scrutiny. This is absolutely true, but private sector employees don't receive their salaries directly from tax dollars, and they certainly aren't endowed with the same level of authority. With great authority comes greater scrutiny and greater responsibility. Law enforcement is granted the statutory authority to deprive individuals of their private liberties and freedoms, either temporarily through arrest powers, or permanently through lethal force, if necessary. Since these powers are only granted to specific individuals, shouldn't the citizenry have the right to demand higher standards of ethics, morality, and integrity of them?

I, personally, believe the public should have such rights. Furthermore, I believe that union representatives should work with police administration rather than against them. It is not uncommon for union representatives to come to the aid of a union member (officer) even though they know what was done was at least inappropriate, if not outright unethical or illegal. I'm all for union representation and protection, but not when the malfeasance of an individual is clearly documented. If an officer violates the law, they should be subject to the same consequences of any other citizen. I could argue that the standard for officers of the law should be higher than the average person.

In other words, I believe compliance to the laws cuts both ways. Citizens are not only expected to obey and follow the laws, orders, and directions of police officers, they are statutorily required to or suffer the consequences. Likewise, police officers are expected to obey and administer those same laws fairly and impartially, and in fact, they are statutorily required to do so. Unfortunately, this isn't always done. Far too often, citizens observe police breaking the law in some way, such as speeding past on the freeway not because of a call, but because they know they can get to wherever they are going quicker because other officers won't stop them. This, in my opinion, is shameful, unacceptable, and unethical. I was in an unmarked police car traveling through Oregon when several marked police cars from the same jurisdiction blew past me while I was traveling the speed limit. I listened to the aerial patrol call out the first vehicle to a unit on the ground that replied, "That's one of ours." This happened two more times before the aerial unit asked if he missed a memo about something going on. The ground unit answered back that there was a drug recognition conference going on in Portland and they were just rushing to get there on time. While this is a fairly minor infraction, it just shows the unwillingness of police administrators to deal with police infractions to the code of ethics, even while the code states officers should be exemplary in obeying the law. Given how blatant these officers were in their actions, I can't imagine someone didn't complain, and even if no public member complained, what type of organizational structure gives multiple officers from the same department the security to feel comfortable in such blatant disregard for the law? There were times in my career when I witnessed what I felt was an excessive use of force during an arrest. In one particular case, when I spoke to the senior officer, he told me

I needed to be more observant because obviously I missed the arrestee attempting to resist. Not satisfied with his answer, I spoke to our sergeant about my concerns and was told to leave it alone, because someday soon I would need that officer to back me up, and if he felt he couldn't trust me his response just might be a little slow, and seconds count when you're getting your ass kicked. His point was clear: you always support your fellow officers or you won't survive in the line of duty. While I'm ashamed to admit it, there were additional times early in my career when I saw what I would suspect to be the onset of excessive force. I'd turn away so I didn't witness whatever occurred so that if questioned, I could honestly say I didn't witness any use of excessive force. The thin blue line was alive and well in my agency, as well. As I rose through the ranks, I clearly explained to those within my scope of supervision that I wouldn't tolerate unethical behavior, and if I could prove such actions were taking place, I would recommend appropriate disciplinary action up to, and including, termination. Correcting the disease of the thin blue line must always start with the head of the agency, and then be infused downward into the lowest levels of the organization. The thin blue line is a slippery slope that, when tolerated within an organization, only accelerates the farther down into the agency it travels. It is unethical behavior at best, and corruption and lawlessness at worst. When the thin blue line is discovered within an agency, the entire agency and everyone working within it are all painted with the same broad brush of community distrust and hostility. When this happens it is unfortunate, because often those officers who would normally work within the agency to correct such behaviors quickly learn that if they don't adjust their behavior and support their fellow officers, there is a real possibility they will be on their own on the streets in a community that distrusts every officer simply because they are wearing the uniform. This is precisely where law enforcement finds itself today. Noble men and women in law enforcement have either been silenced or have changed their behavior in order to maintain their careers, the respect of fellow officers, and their safety on the streets. More often than not, those truly honest, ethical, and caring officers simply leave their department and go to work for another whose policies and procedures are more in line with their views and adhere closer to the code of ethics. However, if they can't find another department, they may leave the profession all together, and that's no solution.

There is another phenomenon that occurs daily that few police administrators fully appreciate, that being "once a cop always a cop." Several years ago, a man was arrested by the Boise Police Department for allegedly dealing methamphetamine. The headline of the local newspaper the next day read, "Former Boise Police Officer Arrested for Dealing Methamphetamine." The most surprising aspect of this headline is that nowhere in the article itself was it pointed out that this individual left the Boise Police Department many, many years earlier.

This only illustrates the extent to which public expectations for officer behavior far surpass that of other professions. As another example, not so many years back if a citizen's portrayal of events differed from that of a police officer's, it was not uncommon for a judge to admonish the citizen and explain that the officer has nothing to gain by not being truthful, whereas the citizen does have a lot to gain. Therefore, since the stories differed but there was no proof one way or the other, the judge would take the officer's word over the citizen's. While I know this still occurs today in courts, I would submit it isn't as prevalent as it once was because too many judges have witnessed untruths or partial truths coming from an officer while testifying. In many courts today, if there is a lack of evidence or documentation, the judge will side with the citizen and dismiss the charge rather than assume the officer is always correct. This is a step in the right direction, as the law clearly states "innocent until proven guilty."

CHAPTER 5

BLACKS LIVES MATTER

"Hands up; Don't Shoot."
-????

The dangerous anti-police rhetoric of the Blacks Lives Matter movement (BLM) has become so volatile and pervasive during protest rallies it has diminished any valid complaint it might have had. The "hands up, don't shoot" rally cry is based on a narrative that has been proven false in the Michael Brown case where the forensic evidence proved Mr. Brown did not have his hands in the air and never said don't shoot, and to continue to promote this error as factual is not only reckless, it's patently dishonest, manipulative, and dangerous towards all citizens as well as police officers.

Even a cursory review of the BLM website clearly demonstrates it is a movement committed to rebuilding the Black Liberation Movement.[41] The Black Liberation movement was rooted in building the new communist party, entrenched in Marxism-Leninism as Mao Tse Tung taught. Anyone dissenting is thought to be intellectually incompetent. Independent thought is rejected and the individual's expression of an opposing view is labeled as a "sell-out" to the capitalistic and imperialistic forces working against true revolution. In fact, when the Communist Party in the United States was advocating the "peaceful transition to socialism" in the late 1960's and early 1970's, it was branded as having "sold-out" the working class in the United States by the Black Panther Party, which at that time was becoming the new

---

[41] Black Lives Matter, About the Black Lives Matter Network, accessed July 8, 2016, http://blacklivesmatter.com/about.

face of revolution. The Black Liberation Movement, the Black Workers' Congress, the Black Panthers, and now the Black Lives Matter movement seek to promote what is seen by its leadership as the 'wisdom' in Stalin's teachings, which centers on the idea "the Party becomes strong by ridding itself of opportunist elements," and Mao Tse Tung's thought that, "Truth develops through its struggle against falsehood. This is how Marxism develops. Marxism develops in the struggle against middle class ideology, and it is only through struggle that it can develop."[42] But history has shown us over and over again it isn't the violent revolutions that create lasting sustainable social reform; instead, it is the peaceful actions of Rosa Parks and Doctor Martin Luther King, where individual intellectual pursuit, opposition, and discussion are not only embraced, but also encouraged.

Given the brief history above, it's not surprising the Black Lives Matter organization seeks to silence any dissenting voice while demanding absolute, unquestioning loyalty of its followers. It must demand an unquestioning following because it is built solely on false premises. Anyone who dares to challenge the factual basis of its founding principles is immediately labeled a "sell-out" to the cause.

From its official website, we can gather their overarching message.

> "#BlackLivesMatter was created in 2012 after Trayvon Martin's murderer, George Zimmerman, was acquitted for his crime, and dead 17-year old Trayvon was posthumously placed on trial for his own murder...Rooted in the experiences of Black people in this country who actively resist our dehumanization, #BlackLivesMatter is a call to action and a response to the virulent anti-Black racism that permeates our society. Black Lives Matter is a unique contribution that goes beyond extrajudicial killings of Black people by police and vigilantes.[43]

> When we say Black Lives Matter, we are broadening the conversation around state violence to include all the ways in which Black people are intentionally left powerless at the hands of the state. We are talking about the ways in which Black lives are deprived of our basic human rights and

---

[42] Encyclopedia of Anti-Revisionism On-Line, "History of the Modern Black Liberation Movement and the Black Workers Congress Summed-Up, Paul Saba, Transcription, Editing and Markup: http://www.marxist.org/history/erol/ncm-1/bwc-history.htm, accessed July 22, 2016.

[43] Black Lives Matter, About The Black Lives Matter Network, accessed July 8, 2016, http://blacklivesmatter.com

dignity.[44]

#BlackLivesMatter is working for a world where Black lives are no longer systematically and intentionally targeted for demise.[45]

We completely expect those who benefit directly and improperly from White supremacy to try and erase our existence. We fight that every day. But when it happens amongst our allies, we are baffled, we are saddened, and we are enraged. And it's time to have the political conversation about why that's not okay."[46]

Let's take a moment and analyze the above statements. According to BLM, George Zimmerman committed a crime, even though he was acquitted by a jury of six women, five of which were white, and one of which was colored, of the charges brought against him. Many have suggested the jury's racial make-up contributed to the acquittal. Yet the very same argument was made about the acquittal of O.J Simpson, with a jury that was made up of eight black women, one black man, one Hispanic man, and two white women. While I will concede that the American judicial system isn't perfect, it does try to be fair and impartial to the accused, and in each of the cases cited above the system worked. These are the words of the Martin family attorney immediately after the conclusion of jury selection: "This case has always been about equal justice. Equal justice under the law is not a black value or a white value. It's an American value. With the makeup of this jury, the question of whether every American can get equal justice regardless of who serves on their jury panel will be answered. We expect the jury pool to do their duty and be fair and impartial."[47] Whether you liked the jury's verdict in either case is irrelevant; it is our system of justice and, as Americans, we must accept the outcome, regardless of personal opinions. The jury is the determiner of facts, and they ruled the way they thought was best in each case. That's how our system works. End of story.

While I'm sure there have been unintentional, and in some cases perhaps

---

[44] Black Lives Matter, About The Black Lives Matter Network, accessed July 8, 2016,

[45] Black Lives Matter, About The Black Lives Matter Network, accessed July 8, 2016, http://blacklivesmatter.com

[46] Black Lives Matter, About The Black Lives Matter Network, accessed July 8, 2016, http://blacklivesmatter.com

[47] Jet Magazine, "All Women Jury Selected in George Zimmerman Trial, June 24, 2013, http://www.jetmag.c/news/all-women-jury-george-zimmerman-case/ accessed July 9, 2016.

intentional, miscarriages of justice within our legal system, I don't believe there is a systemic effort to deprive black people equal justice or basic rights, nor are black people being targeted for systematic demise as suggested by the Black Lives Matter movement.[48] I will agree with BLM in the fact that there have probably been miscarriages of justice involving African-Americans in the past and certainly will be in the future (everyone makes mistakes, even the court system), but the same is true for all races, as disclosed in later chapters. The system isn't perfect, but it is one of the best judicial systems in the entire world.

By and large, the system is truly color blind. The Baltimore case held a significant possibility of racial bias interfering with American justice. The black prosecutor's early statements indicated a potential bias against six officers. At the time of this writing, however, the black judge presiding over all six trials, three black and three white, has acquitted four! After the trial, the prosecutor was accused of violating the officers' constitutional rights by failing to provide defense counsel with exculpatory evidence – as required by law. To me, this shows a fair, impartial and equal treatment of the accused by the court.

However, none of these facts matter to the Black Lives Matter movement. There have been accusations of racism, bigotry, racial profiling, poor prosecution, and unfair rulings. White individuals who point out the fact that George Zimmerman was acquitted, that the forensic evidence has disproven the "hands up, don't shoot" element of the Michael Brown case, and that four of the six Baltimore police officers have been acquitted are quickly labeled as racists. Individuals of African-American descent who disagree with the Black Lives Matter movement are labeled as "Uncle Tom" or "Aunt Jemima," which is as good as being labeled a "sell-out" to imperialism and capitalism or, in BLM's ideology, the white middle class

You see, for this particular movement it's not about a desire to have a political discussion about white supremacy. It's about furthering an ideology of black racism and bigotry, and establishment of a Marxist-Leninist viewpoint in which any opposing view is to be crushed by false accusations. It is a system that demands unquestionable loyalty, no independent thought, and violence to accomplish its goals. It is actually a system that further victimizes blacks and, if it prevails, will result in further violent clashes between people in authority and members of the Black Lives Matter movement. But, in my opinion, the most dangerous component of the Black Lives Matter movement is that it is entirely based on untruths, and fueled

---

[48] Black Lives Matter, About the Black Lives Matter Network, accessed July 8, 2016, http://blacklivesmatter.com.

by the raw emotion of individuals who are taught not to be independent thinkers but rather blind followers of a movement systematically designed to limit personal freedoms, abilities, and accomplishments.

There is indeed room for frank, fact driven discourse about perceived and actual biases in the judicial system, law enforcement, and society, but the fact remains that to bring about lasting change the discourse must be civil, intelligent, and based in facts, not false emotional rhetoric.

CHAPTER 6

MARYLAND VERSUS BRADY

"In the halls of justice, the only justice is found in the halls."
Lenny Bruce

In 1963, the United States Supreme Court in Maryland versus Brady ruled that prosecutors must disclose all exculpatory (favorable to the defendant) evidence and any material evidence that could impact the outcome of the case. This evidence is commonly known as "Brady Material," or "Brady's reach," and includes any evidence in the prosecutor's possession or in the possession of the government that could be used to impeach witnesses, including any payment or promises of leniency any witness may receive in exchange for their testimony. Brady's reach also includes any evidence in the possession of law enforcement, even if that evidence is unknown by the prosecutor at the time.[49]

In a system of justice where the public's trust is placed in the checks and balances established in the judicial system itself, the integrity of those involved is supposed to be above reproach. Ultimate trust is bestowed upon the police officers who enforce the laws, the attorneys who handle the case, and ultimately the courts who hear the case and pronounce judgment. In a system where over ninety-seven percent of the cases are concluded without going to trial,[50] it is critical to the process for those given such high standing

---

[49] The Open File, "Misconduct: Failure to Disclose, accessed July24, 2014,
http://www.prosecutorialaccountability.com/defining-misconduct/failure -to-disclose/

[50] Sunday Review Editorial, "Rampant Prosecutorial Misconduct, The New York Times, January 5, 2014, http://www.nytimes.com/2014/01/05/opinion/sunday/rampant-prosecutorial-

to be above suspicion in their professional morals and integrity.

Unfortunately, just a cursory review United States Supreme Court records reveals this is a process with a systematic integrity problem bordering on complete moral failure. This is both preventable and unnecessary, if each component within the judicial system would conduct themselves with the highest of ethical standards and rigidly follow their respective ethical oaths. Here is a brief history lesson in the *types of failures* mentioned above as outlined by the Open File 2016:

Brady v. Maryland (1963) – Two individuals were accused of murder and faced the death penalty. One of the defendants admitted he was the individual who actually committed the murder, and confirmed the other defendant's involvement. The other defendant admitted he was there, but didn't participate in the murder. *Prosecutors turn over all the statements of the actual murderer, except the one in which the other defendant admits he was present but didn't actually help kill the victim.*

Giglio v. United States (1972) – *The key witness testified he had not received a promise of leniency in return for his testimony even though he actually had.* Although the trial prosecutor didn't know this at trial, the court ruled it was the prosecution's obligation to disclose this fact to the defense.

United States v. Agurs (1976) – Defendant was convicted of murder even though claiming self-defense. *Prosecutors failed to disclose the victim's criminal record* and the court ruled that the prosecution was obligated to disclose such information.

United States v. Bagley (1985) – Prior to trial, Defendant requested the prosecution disclose any "deals, promises, or inducements." *Prosecution failed to disclose the fact that two of their key witnesses were undercover agents for the Bureau of Alcohol, Tobacco, and Firearms.* The court held the prosecution must disclose this for possible impeachment evidence.

Kyles v. Whitley (1995) – Defendant was convicted of murder. *Prior to trial, police had collected eyewitness statements of the attacker's physical description being inconsistent with the defendant's actual physical traits.* These statements were not disclosed to the defense, and the court ruled those statements were required to be disclosed.

Banks v. Dretke (2004) – *Prosecutor failed to disclose that one key witness was a paid government informant and another witness's testimony had been coached, then also failed to correct the record when both witnesses testified falsely.*

Smith v. Cain (2012) – At the trial, the key witness pointed at the defendant and said, "[The murderer] is right there. I'll never forget him." *The same key witness had disclosed, one hour after the killings, that he could not describe*

---

misconduct.html

the intruders and that he had not seen their faces. This fact was not disclosed by the prosecution to the defense.[51]

In January 2014, The New York Times ran an editorial entitled *Rampant Prosecutorial Misconduct* that claimed that according to the "Center for Prosecutor Integrity, multiple studies over the past 50 years show that courts punish prosecutorial misconduct in less than 2 percent of the cases where it occurred." Furthermore, the article also cited the "National Registry of Exonerations, claiming 43 percent of the wrongful convictions are the result of official misconduct." This caused the chief judge for the Ninth Circuit Court of Appeals, Alex Kozinski, to lament, "Some prosecutors don't care about Brady because courts don't make them care."[52] And to continue: "Fighting this official misconduct isn't only about protecting the innocent it…it's about preserving the public's trust in our justice system."[53] Is it any wonder the American public has lost confidence in our judicial system today when every step in the process has experienced perversions of the system? These figures are astounding to me. Just think about that for a moment; nearly 50 percent of innocent people wrongfully convicted of a crime were convicted based on official misconduct. It causes me to wonder just how many uneducated individuals are buffaloed into confessing to a crime simply because they don't know any better.

However, it is extremely important to realize that, while I have been pointing out the failures within the judicial system, I still believe the majority of the system strives to work properly according to ethical standards. The above outlined failures are indeed egregious and since, for the most part, they have gone unpunished, our legal system has entered onto a very slippery slope. This must be corrected immediately, before the over-all corruption found in other parts of government infest the system designed to maintain checks and balances where all individuals are treated fairly and impartially. Yet the disturbing trend of "the end justifies the means" continues because, even if caught, the chances of any significant consequence are so slight there is virtually no professional or personal risk. All too often, those engaged in the judicial system do not actually seek true justice. The fact is, the duty of

---

[51] The Open File, "Misconduct: Failure to Disclose"
http://www.prosecutorialaccountability.com/defining-misconduct/failure -to-disclose/accessed July 24, 2016.

[52] Review Editorial, "Rampant Prosecutorial Misconduct, The New York Times, January 5, 2014, http://www.nytimes.com/2014/01/05/opinion/sunday/rampant-prosecutorial-misconduct.html

[53] Review Editorial, "Rampant Prosecutorial Misconduct, The New York Times, January 5, 2014, http://www.nytimes.com/2014/01/05/opinion/sunday/rampant-prosecutorial-misconduct.html

the police, prosecutor, defense, and court is to seek the truth, and not necessarily a conviction. The absolute truth is what should be sought in any court case, not high conviction statistics. Justice will never be served by depriving people of their due process or sending innocent people to prison.[54] In fact, I would rather see a few guilty individuals go free than ever see one innocent individual wrongly sent to prison.

---

[54] "Discovery under Brady V. Maryland," http://finchmccraine.com, accessed July 24, 2016.

CHAPTER 7

"I'M INNOCENT; THEY'RE NOT EVEN MY PANTS, MAN!"

"The media's the most powerful entity on Earth. They have the power
to make the innocent guilty and the guilty innocent, and that's power.
Because they control the minds of the masses."
Malcolm X

Now, before everyone reading this accuses me of being an idealistic
nitwit, understand that I fully recognize nearly every guilty person claims
innocence when being accused. As a former police officer, detective, and
police administrator, I've heard the guilty profess innocence even when
confronted with evidence proving their guilt. For instance, the above
chapter title comes from an individual I arrested. During the search of this
person, a small bindle of methamphetamine was removed from the front
pocket of the pants the individual was wearing. The first thing he said was,
"I'm innocent; they're not even my pants, man!" This was an interesting turn
of events, considering I had also removed cash from the same pants that the
person claimed *was* theirs, along with their wallet, keys, and other items all
belonging to the person. Then when the methamphetamine was discovered,
suddenly this person was wearing someone else's pants. Now, I suppose it's
possible. But it wasn't very likely, and in this particular case they weren't
someone else's pants. Officers with any time on the job all have similar
stories to tell. But we must remember that not everyone accused of a crime
is guilty. The majority, I believe, are guilty, but there are a few that are
actually innocent. Every police officer will agree that when something is
wrong, their senses alert them to potential danger. I submit that the same is
true when dealing with a truly innocent person. Something within the officer
lets them know something isn't quite right, and it's at this point the officer

must make a decision to either investigate further or stifle this silly little notion. An example of this feeling is the story of a woman who witnessed the suicide of the guy she was dating. The only potential witness in the room was seated on the couch facing away from the arguing couple when the gun was fired. Initially, I was assigned as the secondary investigator on the case with my primary duty being crime scene investigation and reconstruction while the lead investigator handled all interviews. At the conclusion of my investigation, I determined the man had died from a self-inflicted gunshot wound to the head. These findings were further confirmed by the forensic pathologist's autopsy. The family objected to my conclusion and the forensic pathologists report, and requested an independent investigation by the Idaho State Police. All files were turned over to the Idaho State Police, and their detective's initial report indicated the girlfriend murdered the boyfriend and suggested she be charged with the murder. I told them that if they felt it was a murder they could charge her, but I would not. When I asked them what evidence they had based their conclusion on, they told me that the interviews conducted indicated she was lying about the facts of the case. I agreed that she was lying about some of the facts, but also said they couldn't ignore the fact that the forensic evidence revealed she couldn't have murdered the individual. Our two agencies were at a stalemate as to our findings. The Idaho State Police then hired an internationally known blood spatter expert to analyze our findings and perform various tests to determine whether the facts in question indicated murder. After that expert's independent investigation, he confirmed my finding that it was a self-inflicted gunshot wound. Blood spatter proved the girlfriend was standing where she said she was standing when he pulled the trigger, which clearly indicated this wasn't a murder. Yet, years after this case was closed, I was told by the lead investigator that at least one of the state police investigators was telling others in the law enforcement community that I had messed the case up, and the girlfriend got away with murder. I still stick by my conclusion, and had I given in to the enormous pressure applied by the Idaho State Police, that poor woman, who was well known to multiple police agencies, would have been charged and possibly tried for a crime she didn't commit.

All too often, the notion of innocence is stifled, and police individuals pursue the theory established initially, reasoning that if it is wrong somehow the court process will reveal any investigative error. But history forces us into different reasoning. Over the last fifty years, exculpatory and material evidence has been sequestered to convict in some cases, causing nearly 46 percent of the innocent people exonerated (after years in prison) to be exonerated **because of** official misconduct somewhere along the process.[55] It must also be mentioned that some of these exonerations are due to advances in forensic science and not official misconduct. But the fact remains that too many innocent people are spending time in prison for crimes they didn't commit, and it takes individuals with integrity to help prevent this type of travesty. My life would have been so much easier if I had acquiesced to the state police. After all, the girl in question was constantly in trouble with the law, untruthful most the time, and had a lengthy criminal history. She wasn't exactly a good person, but the facts remain, she wasn't a murderer either. To charge her as such would have been wrong and a violation of the Law Enforcement Code of Ethics, if not outright immoral.

I relay this story not for self-exaltation but as an example of how easy it is to be mistaken and attempt to force the facts to fit into the theory, rather than adjusting the theory to fit the actual facts. If this can happen in rural Idaho between one of the largest police agencies and a smaller department, then it happens everywhere.

There is a much more tragic story occurring in rural Idaho in which politicians and law enforcement entities are currently engaged in the police equivalent of "they're not even my pants, man!" Unfortunately, the situation involves the death of a well-known community member. It is a case that has divided a small community and has the potential to ruin the reputation of law enforcement there and in surrounding counties. It involves a police shooting where the lead investigative agency and the state attorney general are pointing fingers at each other and claiming it's not their responsibility to determine the facts. The Idaho State Police is the lead agency and has taken nearly a year to complete the investigation. Their findings are inconclusive. The attorney general recently concluded there are conflicting witness statements, and therefore they have decided not to charge the two officers involved because they cannot prove any case beyond a reasonable doubt. As a former law enforcement professional, I don't intend to critique the investigation, other than to say it is disturbing to me that the state police investigation is inconclusive. Either it was a justified shooting or it wasn't. The family of the deceased, the community, and the officers involved deserve a definitive result. The state police have claimed they are not the lead agency, and the attorney general claims his role is to determine if there is sufficient evidence to pursue criminal charges or not. An inconclusive finding seems to indicate a need for further investigation to determine if this

---

[55] Eugene Volokh, "Judge Kozinski on wrongful convictions and excessively long sentences," The Washington Post, July 15, 2015.

was a justified or questionable officer involved shooting, even if the facts of the case cannot be adequately determined. Yet neither agency has the political will to state a conclusion.

Furthermore, this case is fraught with the appearance of impropriety. Based on documents from the Idaho State Police investigation, both officers involved had serious Brady issues, which has been ignored by both officer's agency heads, the Idaho State Police, and the POST Council. Here I also submit there is a conflict of interest, since the Idaho State Police is the entity which operates the State of Idaho's Peace Officer Standards and Training academies, which in turn are responsible for officer certification and decertification. One officer involved worked as a deputy for the sheriff's department in the same county in which my department was located. I had questioned his integrity in 2010 after a confidential informant suggested the possibility of this officer's distribution of sensitive law enforcement information in a county wide drug investigation. According to the state police documents, the supervising sheriff sought legal advice from the City and County Risk Management Plan and **was advised by one of their attorneys not to investigate the integrity issue**. Their investigation of the officer's integrity was closed and reported as unfounded. Approximately nine months later, the sheriff was contacted by the POST director, who advised the sheriff that this same officer had failed to disclose prior military experience on his POST and county employment applications. According to the state police documents, this officer resigned prior to the department having the chance to address the application inconsistencies.

I also have significant background information on the other officer involved in the shooting, because he was initially hired by me when I was a chief of police. This particular officer's employment was terminated by my agency twenty-one months later, when an internal affairs investigation revealed that he violated several department and city policies, as well as Idaho Fish and Game laws, and Fish and Game issued him several misdemeanor citations. Based on documents obtained via a public information request, this officer was subsequently convicted of two misdemeanor charges and received a withheld judgment. Approximately one month after his dismissal from my department, the Idaho POST and the Office of Professional Responsibility (OPR) initiated a decertification investigation. Approximately two months later, I received a follow-up telephone call from the decertification investigator in which he informed me he believed the officer was being untruthful with him. I provided additional documentation to this investigator and added that if the investigator believed the officer was being untruthful, my personal recommendation would be decertification. In addition, the officer filed a notice of tort claim, alleging the decertification investigator of the Idaho State Police unlawfully disseminated information gleaned from his interview, thereby violating his rights under the Fourth, Fifth, and Eighth Amendments of the Constitution. Approximately two months later, POST OPR agreed to a stipulation to dismiss the decertification complaint with prejudice, and the case was closed. The ultimate result of all this legal action was, in my opinion, that both officers should have been de-certified and no longer employed in law enforcement at the time of the fatal shooting previously mentioned.

The underlying cause of officers being allowed to remain officers even after serious offenses is the industry culture in which many of the moral and ethical failures of individual officers are tolerated or downright overlooked by police administrators, POST directors, and decertification boards. From my perspective, nothing violates the Law Enforcement Code of Ethics more clearly or is more frustrating than conducting a thorough internal affairs investigation that clearly demonstrates the officers in question were dishonest, only to be told by the decertification investigator that they will not be recommending decertification because they don't believe the District Court will support the removal of the officers' employment rights given the circumstances. This is despite the fact that Idaho Administrative Code IDAPA 11.11.03 clearly delineates that "the [POST] Council shall decertify any officer who ... willfully or otherwise falsifies or omits any information to obtain any certified status; or violates any of the standards of conduct as established by the council's code of conduct or code of ethics as adopted and amended by the council."[56] Furthermore, IDAPA 11.11.04(d) requires that an officer "not lie, give misleading statements, or falsify written or verbal communications in official reports ... where it is reasonable to expect such information may be relied upon because of position or departmental affiliation."[57] Additionally, the Law Enforcement Code of Ethics clearly forbids officers or police administrators from engaging in acts of dishonesty, whether by thought or deed, in either their official or personal life. Police officers are required to enforce the law without cowardice or favoritism, are prohibited to participate in or encourage acts of corruption, are required not

---

[56] Idaho Administrative Code, (2010) IDAPA 11.11.01 - Rules of the Idaho Peace Officer Standards & Training Council (POST), pp. 23-24, [Online] Available From: http://www.idaho-post.org/rulesnregs/AdminRules.html (Accessed 25 January 2011).

[57] Idaho Administrative Code, (2010) IDAPA 11.11.01 - Rules of the Idaho Peace Officer Standards & Training Council (POST), pp. 23-24, [Online] Available From: http://www.idaho-post.org/rulesnregs/AdminRules.html (Accessed 25 January 2011).

to submit to bribery, and especially are expected not to overlook such acts when they are committed by fellow officers. Every refusal to take corrective action on the part of the police administrator or state certifying agency undermines the value of the Code of Ethics. Every circumstance of alleged officer malfeasance contains nuisances which often prevent the literal interpretation of the Law Enforcement Code of Ethics or the officer's organizational code of conduct. The problem isn't on an individual basis, where the code of ethics is analyzed and used to decertify officers for malfeasance. It is the profession's reluctance, if not outright refusal, to enforce the spirit of their ethical code. Each refusal to take appropriate action violates the code of ethics' principles in a profession where success relies upon relationships with citizens as a means of building loyalty and trust. The profession's problem of cover-ups and rationalizations for officer malfeasance has become so pervasive that a strict adherence to the standards law enforcement professes to abide by has become merely an obstacle for police administrators, POST directors, and decertification board members trying to justify their decisions. Developing excuses for inaction rather than taking the appropriate corrective action is tantamount to endorsement of the unethical behavior(s).

CHAPTER 8

SO WHERE DO WE GO FROM HERE?

"The secret of change is to focus all of your energy, not on fighting the old, but on building the new."
- Socrates

Having spent much of this book focusing on all the problems associated with the American judicial system, I'd like to shift the focus and begin to offer possible solutions.

It is clear that law enforcement must shift its paradigms away from its current 'thin blue line' approach to ethics, morality, and politics and develop a new and innovative approach. This approach must be the new mandate industry wide to reverse the ever-swelling tide of public distrust, cynicism, and negative word of mouth responses to police actions. By devising a nationwide strategy through the POST Directors, I believe law enforcement's reputation and public image can be significantly improved over the next decade. The strategy would have a state-specific implementation structure involving the use of intermediary disciplinary procedures, to include public censures and certification suspension for officer malfeasance, tied to adherence of the universally accepted standards in the Law Enforcement Code of Ethics. While it is clear the current methodology employed in officer decertification isn't entirely effective, advancements in police decertification procedures have been made with a great deal of validity and progressive planning. These advancements, pointed out by Goldman, Puro, and Smith, have resulted in significant change and improvements for the law enforcement profession in the United States in the last two decades. The following recommendations are meant to not only build upon and enhance the progress accomplished in the area of police officer malfeasance, but also enhance the professions' public image, branding, and organizational reputations.

Law enforcement's primary approach for officer malfeasance has consisted of two prongs. Initially, the officer's employing organization has a duty to address, train, remediate, discipline, and report officer malfeasance to the state certifying agency, POST. The administrator of the officer's organization should be responsible for investigating, analyzing, and reporting the organization's findings and disciplinary procedures utilized. The police administrator also must indicate whether the organization wishes to recommend officer decertification to the POST director. However, regardless of the police administrator's recommendations, POST's professional standards division is responsible for reviewing the officer's actions, and determining if POST will instigate a decertification investigation based on such a review. If POST determines the intention to pursue decertification of the officer, the police administrator is notified in writing. At this point, there is potential for conflict between the certifying agency and the police administrator. In some cases, the two parties agree, but in others, the administrator feels their organization has addressed the malfeasance correctly, and the certifying agency is pursuing additional sanctions contrary to the administrator's recommendations; and, occasionally, the administrator's recommendation is for stronger action than POST deems appropriate.

A simple way to correct this potentially adversarial dynamic while simultaneously enhancing stakeholder trust is to require officer disciplinary actions to become a matter of public record. Simply removing the exception from the public open records law that is granted to personnel matters (like disciplinary actions) as it pertains to police personnel, or any other public sector employee whose salary is funded at or in excess of 50% by tax revenues, would accomplish this goal. This approach becomes beneficial from a public and political transparency perspective and would significantly minimize police administrators from hiding police malfeasance within their own organizations. While it is recognized this proposal may inflame the ire of some police services personnel,[58] one must not forget that the purpose of such rules are to reduce the opportunities for officers to violate the public's trust.[59] In a system of transparency, it wouldn't matter whether the

---

[58] Gerald A. Summers, "Law Enforcement Decertification: Shifting the Paradigms of Ethics, Morality, And Politics from Law Enforcements' Traditional Approach to A Resource-based View" MBA diss., University of Liverpool, 2011.

[59] Puro, S., & Goldman, R., & Smith, W., (1997) 'Police decertification: changing patterns among the

betrayal came from an individual officer, police administrator, or entire organization, because the way it was handled would be public record. Furthermore, since police services are funded primarily from taxpayer revenues, the public has the right to information about people and events paid for with taxpayer money.[60] According to Sir Robert Peel, the ability of police services to function appropriately in performance of their duties requires the publics' approval of law enforcement actions.[61] Some administrators might object on the basis that public disclosure of disciplinary actions might prejudice members of the community against the disciplined officer. It is true that it very well might, but that fact would have been fully disclosed to the individual officer upon their affirmation of the Law Enforcement Code of Ethics. The officer clearly accepted this public scrutiny potential when he/she agreed to keep their private life unsullied and to live as an example to others in regards to compliance with the law. Once again, the public trust and statutory authority bestowed upon police officers requires a higher standard of performance. For those not wishing to be subjected to such public scrutiny, there is always the option of choosing a different career path.

There is obviously a huge disparity between states as to what constitutes moral turpitude, and an even greater gap in enforcement. The belief of both police administrators and POST directors seems to be that if intermediary steps were statutorily provided to POST directors and decertification boards, it would promote greater enforcement of the code of ethics. In theory, this would force greater compliance to the code of ethics by commissioned police services personnel. For instance, in most states, a police officer convicted of the misdemeanor offense of driving while under the influence of alcohol, rarely results in the officer's decertification, and discipline is left solely up to the determination of the officer's agency. While some police organizations will discipline appropriately, others will not. By establishing public records disclosure and the certifying agency's statutorily approved right to intermediary processes, like public censures of police officers and the ability to suspend an officer's certification, we could provide

---

states, 1985-1995' *Policing: an International Journal of Police Strategies & Management*, 20 (3), pp. 481-496.

[60] Gerald A. Summers, "Law Enforcement Decertification: Shifting the Paradigms of Ethics, Morality, And Politics from Law Enforcements' Traditional Approach to A Resource-based View" MBA diss., University of Liverpool, 2011.

[61] Bloy, M., (2010) 'Sir Robert Peel's Nine Points of Policing', *A Web of English History*, [Online] Available From: http://www.historyhome.co.uk/peel/laworder/9points.htm (Accessed 3 March 2011).

the opportunity for POST decertification boards to hold officers accountable when their police organizations choose not to. For example, with an officer's first DUI conviction a public censure via local media outlets should result. A second DUI conviction could result in a minimum 90- to 180-day certification suspension and mandatory counseling. A third DUI conviction could result in automatic decertification.

Other misdemeanor convictions might require immediate decertification. For example, domestic violence convictions involving the use of physical force, thefts, dishonesty in an official capacity, perjury, and false or misleading statements in police reports, investigations, or courtroom testimony are all clearly violations of the moral turpitude clause in the Law Enforcement Code of Ethics and the police organization's Code of Conduct. Each violation and the corresponding circumstances must be thoroughly investigated and analyzed, and the findings and corresponding actions or sanctions must be open for the publics' review if law enforcement is to regain the media and the publics' trust.

Routine complaints against individual officers typically revolve around the officer's actions, such as issuing a ticket the recipient didn't feel was warranted, or the officer's demeanor, as when the officer didn't smile, or their words were harsh and not appreciated. In most police services organizations, these complaints are handled at the patrol sergeant's level. Often, these sergeants have little or no training in customer service or conflict resolution. Patrol sergeants are tasked with many competing functions regarding personnel supervision. Because of these competing functions, when a non-criminal officer complaint is received it is a low priority and often isn't addressed immediately, which can make the complainant feel unimportant. However, if it is handled immediately, the complainant may feel rushed, or as if their objection to the officer's actions fell on deaf ears. Marketing studies continue to demonstrate that less than ten percent of those receiving a service actually complain.[62] Those doing the complaining are generally individuals in higher socioeconomic positions and tend to be more versed in the service protocols. On the other hand, when individuals perceive they possess a lack of power in a particular circumstance, they tend not to voice their complaint. Furthermore, when a complaint is logged people expect to be treated fairly. When these individuals sense they were not treated fairly, reactions become immediate,

---

[62] Gerald A. Summers, "Law Enforcement Decertification: Shifting the Paradigms of Ethics, Morality, And Politics from Law Enforcements' Traditional Approach to A Resource-based View" MBA diss., University of Liverpool, 2011.

volatile, and long lasting, if not permanent.[63] Because patrol sergeants are extremely busy, they often appear uninterested, detached, and gruff to the citizen who feels they have a valid complaint. The system further collapses when the patrol sergeant, wishing to move on to a 'more important' task, tells the complaining party to take it to court, because that's how the system works.

Analyzing this exchange in this light, we see how quickly customer relationships can break down. Police service organizations are very adept at shifting the balance of power away from the complainant and onto themselves, effectively minimizing the citizen, and the negative results of doing such can be seen all around the United States. In order for law enforcement to reverse this swell of community and media hostility, the industry needs to implement effective systems that give community members a way to have their complaints heard by police personnel that are trained in customer service. Community opinions need to be actively solicited by police organizations and implemented in their service procedures. Service failures must be addressed immediately in a transparent manner, with open honest communication in keeping with a service organization. If the organization was wrong, administrators need to admit the organization's failure and accept responsibility. These simple steps on the part of police administrators and organizations will vastly improve the organization's and industry's reputation as a responsive, trustworthy profession.

Perhaps the greatest thing needed for police service organizations in the United States is critical evaluation in an open, unbiased manner. Police administrators need to recognize that police services are not closed systems with limited input from outside sources. In fact, police service organizations are actually open systems in which a vast amount of input is received. Learning to manage this flow of information within this context, and having the strength and moral conviction to confront criminal and ethical failures within their own organization, is required to improve public trust. Developing the political will for transparency in decertification procedures and demanding adherence to the profession's code of ethics, coupled with effective and adequate discipline for those individuals refusing to comply with these standards will result in the organization and its leaders earning the publics' trust back.

Shifting the dynamic in law enforcement away from its traditional approach is a complex and enormously intricate task. Just establishing a

---

[63] Lovelock, C., & Wirtz, J., (2007) Services Marketing: People, Technology, Strategy, Sixth Edition. New Jersey: Pearson Prentice Hall.

viable customer service system for police decertification nationwide is overwhelming, as it involves convincing police administrators, POST directors, legislators, and decertification board members to participate. These issues are further complicated by generational cohorts in which police administrators and middle management often fall into multiple different categories. Currently, most police administrators fall into the Baby Boomer cohort, those born between 1946 and 1964. Baby Boomers tend to be highly competitive and focused on promotion and wealth accumulation. Middle management is different, tending to fall within the Gen Xers cohort, born between 1965 and 1976, and the Millennial's cohort, born between 1977 and 1999. Gen Xers tend to distrust major institutions and are skeptical and cynical in their worldview. Millennial's tend to be technologically proficient, socially concerned, value sensitive, and practical. While these differing cohorts aren't diametrically opposed to one another, their differences are significant enough to create dissension within any organization. Couple this with the traditional top-down hierarchy established by the "me" generation of the Baby Boomers willing to conform (because conformance is viewed as the pathway to promotion and wealth accumulation) with the cynicism and skeptical nature of Gen Xers and socially concerned, value sensitive, practical, technological approach of the Millennial's, and you have a melting pot of ideas and philosophical approaches. However, these generational cohort differences do not have to hinder internal communication. These differences indicate the need for establishing common ground so the internal principles will not be negatively impacted by generational cohorts. Working together can provide an opportunity for police administrators to build upon the strengths of each cohort to develop a synergistic approach to organizational reputation, public image, and branding.[64]

In analyzing and applying business practices to the law enforcement profession, it is essential to understand that the primary purpose is to develop and then maintain positive interaction between citizens and law enforcement. This is necessary for the express purpose of developing loyalty from the community by establishing a high value on law enforcement for the citizen, which can be developed into a positive, life-long interaction.[65] Law enforcement must understand and embrace the fact that it doesn't

---

[64] Gerald A. Summers, "Law Enforcement Decertification: Shifting the Paradigms of Ethics, Morality, And Politics from Law Enforcements' Traditional Approach to A Resource-based View" MBA diss., University of Liverpool, 2011.

[65] King, S., (2007) 'Citizens as customers: Exploring the future of CRM in UK local government', *Government Information Quarterly*, 24 (1), pp. 47-63.

operate in a vacuum, nor will it be allowed to operate with the autonomy it's had in the past. Citizens, as customers, are demanding accountability in all aspects of government, and the most visible element in local government is police services. While the concept of customer loyalty is foreign to most police administrators, it is the business model which has worked in the private sector markets, and it needs to not be ignored by the public sector any longer. Research further suggests that public sector customer relationship management should incorporate three interconnected functions, with each function built upon the other. It should begin with "improving accessibility," previously referred to as transparency, then continue into "organizational transformation," which changes the way law enforcement has traditionally provided its service to the community, and finally end with seeking and utilizing customer input and feedback, which ultimately transforms into "service delivery innovation" and becomes a major transformation within law enforcement.[66]

Throughout the years, the law enforcement profession has developed the self-serving view that it knows what is best for the community and therefore has developed programs around its own worldview. Unfortunately, the community often doesn't view the circumstances in the same manner or from the same perspective as law enforcement. Typically, the breakdown occurs because police services administrators do not understand the business principles and models set forth earlier, and so they see community involvement as a means for the citizenry to force their views of policing strategy and practices onto law enforcement. That is not how it should work, however.

What customer relationship management seeks to receive is customer loyalty and service improvement via enlightened and productive interactions between the customer and service provider. Police administrators need to fully understand seeking and receiving citizen input does not remove their ability or authority to conduct police services according to proper police protocols, which are focused on officer safety and valid tactical approaches. What the public wants is not to tell law enforcement how to conduct their operating protocols with regards to day to day enforcement actions; they are simply seeking transparency and education as to why certain protocols are conducted the way they are. When the public sees multiple police vehicles on a traffic stop, they see that presence of police officers as over-bearing

---

[66] King, S., (2007) 'Citizens as customers: Exploring the future of CRM in UK local government', *Government Information Quarterly*, 24 (1), pp. 47-63.

and excessive, whereas the officers are simply following protocol. The key element the public is missing is why the use of three police vehicles is needed to conduct a felony traffic stop. If the public had this element, they would understand these requirements are necessary and essential for officer safety. Through this example, we see that transparency is a requirement, and it is critical throughout police services to provide a basis on which customer education is conducted. The education of key stakeholders and business leaders is a major component of successful customer relationship management. It has been my professional experience that taking time to meet with and educate the media, elected officials, and key stakeholders in the community has forged strong alliances out of previously staunch opponents, developed trust for the police organization, improved community support for maintaining funding when other departments in the municipality were experiencing cut-backs, and resulted in improved employee morale, because the frontline officer experiences support during their interactions with the media and local business owners.

Utilizing established business strategies of customer relationship management resulted in a competitive advantage over other departments within the same municipality and sustained adequate funding for the police services within the community. Having done the tedious, often difficult, work of educating elected officials through countless workshops on the functions of the police department and the necessity for a specific level of staffing due to officer safety concerns, I can say from experience that it improved the organization's previously tarnished reputation and established goodwill. Meeting with the local media and developing trust and rapport allows police administrators to share more details "off the record" about on-going investigations in order for the media to understand the background, which enables them to cover the story with a more in-depth perspective. Also as a benefit of this newly developed trust, law enforcement is better able to tell its own story, build community support and trust, and develop a reputation for honesty, integrity, and moral standing. With the improved organizational reputation, fewer citizen complaints are lodged against officers, and employee morale is improved. With the improved morale, individual officers take it upon themselves to ensure citizen satisfaction with the calls they handle. Hence, the organization receives the benefits associated with an innovative customer relationship management focus and business model in which the frontline officers take it upon themselves to ensure customer satisfaction, thereby consistently earning the publics' trust and improving organizational branding, public image, and reputation. In effect, what started at the top to improve relationships begins to be handled at lower and lower levels.

Nationwide, law enforcement faces several unique challenges to shift paradigms from its traditional approach. There is a need for legislative changes to the state Public Records Law which currently exempts personnel records and professional discipline from disclosure. As I've said, I would recommend that all public employees who receive 50% or more of their salary, either directly or indirectly, from tax revenues should have all professional discipline subjected to public disclosure.

Currently, sheriffs elected within Idaho do not have to possess POST certification to hold their elected position, while all police chiefs must be POST certified. This creates issues from a decertification standpoint, with Idaho POST currently having little or no recourse against a standing sheriff for violations of the Law Enforcement Code of Ethics. By removing this loophole and subjecting all police administrators to the same ethical standards, improvements can be made to the decertification protocols, thereby improving law enforcement's reputation. In my opinion, POST must have the ability to regulate and sanction all officer malfeasance and code of ethics violations uniformly. Police administrators, whether elected or appointed, need to be held to the same standards as individual officers in terms of ethics, morality, and politics in order to maintain the code of ethics. Granting POST the authority necessary to impose such standards when police administrators fail to do so, coupled with public record law improvements, allows for political transparency, citizen involvement, and greater scrutiny of law enforcement's disciplinary processes. Finally, granting POST statutory authority to issue public censures and impose certification suspensions develops a multi-agency review process for police malfeasance.[67]

---

[67] Gerald A. Summers, "Law Enforcement Decertification: Shifting the Paradigms of Ethics, Morality, And Politics from Law Enforcements' Traditional Approach to A Resource-based View" MBA diss., University of Liverpool, 2011.

CHAPTER 9

OPEN PROSECUTION FILES

"A lack of transparency results in distrust and
a deep sense of insecurity."
Dalai Lama

In keeping with the multi-agency review process, we have seen over the last fifty years, the checks and balances set-up within the American jurisprudence system have also failed because of a lack of transparency. The system was initially established to have the police keep citizens safe from criminals, prosecutors to keep the citizens safe from overzealous police actions, defense attorneys to keep the accused safe from overzealous prosecutors, and judges to insure all of these components followed the law. Ultimately the courts, through judicial reviews, were to hold any wayward elements within the justice system accountable for any violations of individual liberties.

As the United States Supreme Court has noted, the prosecutor represents "a sovereignty whose obligation to govern impartially is as compelling as its obligation to govern at all; and whose interest, therefore, in a criminal prosecution is not that it shall win a case, but that justice shall be done." (Berger v. United States (1935) 295 U.S. 78, 88 [55 S.Ct. 629, 633; 79 L.Ed. 1314, 1321].).[68] This can be in direct opposition to their own professional goals, where higher conviction rates mean higher personnel ratings and potential for high paying positions.

Additionally, since the Brady versus Maryland decision in 1963, we have

---

[68] Prosecutorial Misconduct.com, accessed August 9, 2014, http://www.prosecutorialmisconduct.com.

seen a systematic failure in that, according to the National Registry of Exonerations, 46% of the 1,576 people exonerated since 1989 were exonerated as a result of official misconduct.[69] Here are just two examples from California:

In the Gary Masse case, Masse named Gloria Killian as his accomplice to a robbery to gain leniency in his murder case. In a subsequent investigation years later, after Killian was convicted, this undisclosed leniency agreement was discovered, along with a letter written by Masse to the District Attorney in which he confessed, "I lied my ass off for you people." By the time all of this had been discovered Killian had spent sixteen years in prison, and the prosecutor on the case, even after not correcting the record, walked away with only an admonishment from the California State Bar Association.[70]

Then, in March 2014, California Judge "Thomas Goethals issued an order disqualifying the entire Orange County District Attorney's Office, including all of its two hundred and fifty prosecutors, from continuing to prosecute a major death penalty case … concluding in hiding exculpatory evidence, and then covering up the whole mess, the District Attorney has a conflict of interest in this case, which has actually deprived this defendant of due process in the past." To wrap up his order, Judge Goethals wrote, "It is now apparent that the discovery situation in this case is far worse than the court previously realized. In fact, a wealth of potentially relevant discovery material – an entire computerized data base built and maintained by the Orange County Sheriff over the course of many years which is a repository for information related directly to the very issues that this court was examining as a result of the defendant's motion – remained secret, despite numerous specific discovery orders by this court, until long after the initial evidentiary hearing in this case was concluded and rulings were made."[71]

Since his ruling, Judge Goethals has been the subject of mass disqualification requests by the Orange County District Attorney's Office, which is allowed to request disqualifications without citing a reason. This practice is commonly referred to as "blanket papering," and it puts a strain on the court system as other judges are required to pick up the additional

---

[69] Honorable Alex Kozinski, "Criminal Law 2.0", 44 Geo. L.J. Ann. Rev. Crim. Proc. (2015) iii-Xliv.

[70] Eugene Volokh, "Judge Kozinski on wrongful convictions and excessively long sentences," The Washington Post, July 15, 2015.

[71] Dahlia Lithwick, "You're All Out,"Slate.com, http://www.slate.com/articles/news_and_politics/jurisprudence/2015/orange_county_pro..., accessed August 5, 2016.

cases. It also puts a strain on Judge Goethals' relationships with his peer judges. Two of the three Fourth District Court of Appeal justices ruled in July of 2016 that "...prosecutors have the right to disqualify a judge without providing an explanation," based on a state Supreme Court ruling.[72] Even though the prosecutor's office denied that they were blanket papering Judge Goethals, one of the three Court of Appeals justices felt it was precisely because of his disqualifying of the county prosecutor's office that he was being targeted. Meanwhile, the California Attorney General had already appealed Judge Goethals ruling in this case claiming that "the Orange County prosecutors did nothing wrong in the Dekraai case and that the local sheriff's deputies are to blame for misleading the court about records kept on jailhouse informants."[73] Attorney General Harris further claimed through a spokesperson, "The courts order recusing the entire District Attorney's Office from this case lacks legal justification and must be appealed," adding that "the attorney general will conduct an independent investigation into allegations that the DA's office obstructed justice by withholding evidence."[74] Many in California are questioning the ability of the attorney general to remain unbiased because of her appeal of the court's ruling as lacking legal justification, while simultaneously conducting an investigation of the prosecutors for alleged misconduct. John Van de Kamp, the former California Attorney General from 1983 to 1991, believes the current attorney general is more interested in saving convictions than in rebuking local prosecutors for misconduct. "The mindset I see is to try to uphold district attorneys in any way possible."[75]

A quick survey of the American Bar Association's Model Rules of Professional Conduct clearly reveals violations of their set standards found in the above-mentioned cases. More specifically, "Rule 8.4 Misconduct – It is professional misconduct for a lawyer to: (c) engage in conduct involving

[72] City News Service, "Orange County DA's office can disqualify Dekraai case judge in murder trial, justices rule," July 26, 2016, accessed August 7, 2016, http://www.presstelgram.com/general-news/20167226orange-county-das-office-can-disqu...

[73] Tony Saavedra, "Kamala Harris' two roles – state's top cop and Senate candidate-leave Dekraai case in limbo," June 1, 2016, http:www.ocregister.com/articles/harris-717932-county-office.html.

[74] Matt Ferner, "California AG Appeals Booting of Orange County DA from Mass Murder Case over Misconduct Allegations," March 20, 2015, accessed August 7, 2016, http://www.huffingtonpost.com/2015/03/20/scott;dekarri-case_n_6911258.html.

[75] Tony Saavedra, "Kamala Harris' two roles – state's top cop and Senate candidate-leave Dekraai case in limbo," June 1, 2016, http:www.ocregister.com/articles/harris-717932-county-office.html.

dishonesty, fraud, deceit or misrepresentation; (d) engage in conduct that is prejudicial to the administration of justice."[76]

At this point, I think it's important to clarify that I am not an attorney. I'm simply an individual who, looking at the literal interpretation of the stated rules of the American Bar Association for misconduct, cannot conceive of how any ethical organization can conclude the actions taken in the Masse case don't rise to a level of extreme professional misconduct worthy of something greater than an admonishment. Even if the district attorney was unaware of Mr. Masse lying on the stand, there was a moral and ethical responsibility to fix such a mistake by disclosing Mr. Masse's letter to the court. The Office of the District Attorney's refusal to disclose this fact resulted in a woman spending sixteen years in prison based upon false testimony. That is a shame at best and criminal at worst, and the attorney or attorneys who were aware of this letter and buried it, in my estimation, should have been disbarred at the very least.

In the Dekraai case, Laura Fernandez of Yale Law School, who studies prosecutorial misconduct, says "It's amazing that both the sheriff's office and the DA's office worked together to cover up the misconduct: 'what really sets Orange County apart is the massive cover-up by both law enforcement and prosecutors- a cover-up that appears to have risen to the level of perjury and obstruction of justice."[77] And yet the California Attorney General defends the prosecutor's office while simultaneously conducting an internal investigation. This is the equivalent of the Orange County Sheriff's Office conducting its own internal affairs investigation to determine any wrong doing after years of organizational corruption has just been revealed. Is it any wonder the general public is losing its trust in the American jurisprudence community and process? How can departments who allow corruption to continue for years be trusted to investigate themselves?

While I have exposed two egregious, extreme cases in California, I submit they are not exclusive to the State of California, and that these types of misconduct occur in both rural and metropolitan communities throughout the United States. Along with all of those is the alleged

---

[76] American Bar Association, "Model Rules For Professional Conduct," accessed August 7, 2016, http://www.americanbar.org/aba.html

[77] Dahlia Lithwick, "You're All Out,"Slate.com, http://www.slate.com/articles/news_and_politics/jurisprudence/2015/orange_county_pro..., accessed August 5, 2016.

prosecutorial misconduct of Marilyn Mosby, the Baltimore City Prosecutor who brought charges without credible evidence, against six Baltimore City Police Officers in the death of Freddie Gray. After several acquittals, Mosby was forced to abandon charges against the remaining officers and is now the subject of disciplinary action and faces potential disbarment. However, given the pathetic history of the courts in the last fifty years regarding prosecutorial misconduct, I don't expect to see anything other than an extremely low level discipline imposed on any unethical prosecutor, including Mosby. It is apparent that the final checks and balances in the American judicial system have failed, leaving corruption to run wild.

In the 1976 ruling in the Imbler versus Pachtman case, the United States Supreme Court ruled, according to the Honorable Alex Kozinski, that "...prosecutors cannot be held liable, no matter how badly they misbehave, for actions such as withholding exculpatory evidence, introducing fabricated evidence, knowingly presenting perjured testimony and bringing charges for which there is no credible evidence. All are immune from liability."[78] The Courts have had the potential to reverse this ruling in light of fifty-plus years of Brady violations, the Masse Case, and the Orange County District Attorney's office scandal.

So, what are some possible solutions to minimize such occurrences from becoming an acceptable pattern in the American justice system? I suggest a three-pronged approach as a possible solution. First, prosecutors should be required to have an open file policy where all potential evidence must be disclosed to the defense, whether the prosecutor intends to use it or not. The same holds true for all potential witnesses. Potential Brady issues must also be disclosed, and can be argued before the judge outside of any juror's purview. Second, the exemption for disclosure of personnel actions should be removed. That would allow the public the ability to judge for themselves whether proper management supervision is being exercised by the elected district or prosecuting attorney. Finally, remove absolute immunity for prosecutors, and have it follow the qualified immunity of police officers. This would open prosecutors up to civil liability for willful misconduct and gross negligence in the performance of their duties, thereby holding them accountable for their actions in and out of the courtroom.

---

[78] Honorable Alex Kozinski, "Criminal Law 2.0", 44 Geo. L.J. Ann. Rev. Crim. Proc. (2015) iii-Xliv.

CHAPTER 10

JUDICIAL OVERSIGHT

"Be as you wish to seem."
Socrates

It must now be apparent that the concept of self-policing is no longer a viable option, as it has failed with law enforcement, prosecutors, defense attorneys, and the courts. There has been reluctance among judges to take a hard stand against misconduct on the part of police officers, attorneys, and other judges, and the result is a corrupted judicial system from top to bottom. Safeguards established long ago have been abandoned for political correctness and systematic expediency, rather than justice. The number of cases involving official misconduct is relatively small in comparison to all cases tried. Still, the fact that 46% of exonerations since 1989 have been due to wrongful convictions as a result of misconduct proves there is a reason for lack of public trust in the system. Add to that the question of how many others have been wrongfully convicted and haven't had their innocence discovered (possibly because exculpatory evidence was destroyed) and the reason for lack of public trust increases dramatically. No one, at this point, can put a definitive number to it, because the closed-off judicial system doesn't allow for a thorough examination of all the evidence.

Given the system failures exposed thus far are numerous enough and disturbing enough to shock the conscience of society, I believe the strongest protection against any type of internal corruption is full public disclosure. Take away the public disclosure exemptions in all states, forcing police administrators, certification agencies, prosecutors, and judges to come out from behind the cloak of secrecy and have their actions, results, and management decisions exposed to the light of public scrutiny. There is a tendency in most organizations or systems to hide that which is unlikely to create a public relations nightmare, when in reality it's always best to expose the system failure, study, and then correct the problem so that it doesn't mushroom into a complete loss of trust towards the organization. This, unfortunately, is where I believe the American jurisprudence system finds itself today, and the only real fix is for each component within the system to perform its appropriate roles and address any failure to do this publicly.

The other alternative I see is to either enforce or discard all ethical oaths. If law enforcement isn't going to be held to the high level of integrity demanded by its code of ethics, then discard it with the caveat, "citizen beware." If prosecutors and defense attorneys aren't going to be held to the standard of their code of ethics, then let's remove the illusion that one actually exists. Finally, if the courts aren't going to be the final check and balance of all that is involved in justice, let's abandon the promise of fairness and justice for all. Even if that won't be the case any longer, at least everyone won't be under any false pretenses.

I believe the solution is a simple one, but it certainly isn't an easy one. Those of us at a professional level must demand and adhere to a moral code; an established standard, if you will, that does not need to be created for it already exists and it is found in the Code of Ethics of each profession. A strict adherence to the spirit found in each code, and the unbiased demand for its enforcement regardless of position, social status, wealth, or politics has the power to correct the corrupted system known as the American Jurisprudence System in less than two decades. Failure to do so will push us ever faster down the destructive path we have created and will eventually lead to anarchy.

CHAPTER 11

CALL TO ACTION

"What you do speaks so loud that I cannot hear what you say."
Ralph Waldo Emerson

Hopefully at this point, you're agreeing with me and wondering how you can be part of the solution. On my website, www.JerrySummersAuthor.com you will find a link to information regarding state laws for release of personnel actions. Each state is different. You can review your state information, and determine if you're in agreement. For instance, Idaho's reads:

M. Personnel records.

Personnel records are only partially open to the public, as provided in Idaho Code § 9-340C(1). In *Federated Publications Inc. v. Boise City*, 128 Idaho 459, 915 P.2d 21 (1996) the Idaho Supreme Court held that the term "applicant" in the provision of public records laws exempting from disclosure certain personnel information refers to an applicant for a position as a public employee. The Court noted that the exemption does not apply to applicants for appointment to vacancies in the city council. *Id.* The Court also found that administrative review of a police shooting incident, which reviewed policies and training and determined completeness of internal discipline procedures was not exempt from disclosure under the public records laws under Idaho Code § 9-340C(1). *Id.* More recently, in *Cowles Publishing Co v. Kootenai Co. Bd. of Commissioners*, 144 Idaho 259, 159 P.3d 896 (2007), the Idaho Supreme Court rejected an argument that e-mail messages, of a personal nature, sent between an elected public official and a public employee were exempt personnel records. The Court held "although the e-mails may be a form of correspondence, they are not the type of communication the legislature meant to exempt in Idaho Code § 9-340C(1).

. . . The legislature meant to exempt only those types of correspondence typically found in a personnel file – for instance, a letter of recommendation, formal correspondence between a superior and employee, or a letter commenting favorably or disfavorably on an employee's professional conduct." Id., 144 Idaho at 264-265. Personnel records have been a frequent point of conflict between public agencies and persons requesting such information.[79]

Based on this, I would choose to write to my state senators and congressmen, requesting full release of personnel records for individuals whose salaries are paid using 50% or more tax dollars.

There are also sample letters for soliciting changes, and links to names of state legislators.

Working together, we can make a difference.

---

[79] http://www.rcfp.org/idaho-open-government-guide/iv-record-categories-open-or-closed/m-personnel-records

www.ingramcontent.com/pod-product-compliance
Lightning Source LLC
Chambersburg PA
CBHW050606280326
41933CB00011B/1997